XUYING

Hello 你好

實用英語教學（第一冊）

教學DVD及書全套教材共54課

丁慧　　李仁德

最新加插英語正確閱讀與發音

專爲華人設計　眞人實景拍攝　輕輕鬆鬆學英語

新唐人電視台
New Tang Dynasty Television

作者的話

在北美有這樣一個群體，他們為了架設中美加文化橋樑，服務造福北美華人社會，利用他們自己的業餘時間和金錢，憑著他們的熱情，技術和善念創辦了第一家獨立非營利華語公共電視台 -- 新唐人電視台，並於 2002 年 2 月在美國開播。新唐人電視台像一股清流，漸漸地流到了北美華人的家裏，我們也很榮幸地成為了這個電視台中的成員。

2001 年年底，電視台的朋友給我們打電話，問我們是否可以幫忙做個英語教學節目。這個節目的目的是幫助在北美不懂英語的華人學會英語。他們有的是剛來北美的，有的是來了多年的。由於不懂英語，給他們在北美的生活增加了很大的困難。我們雖然都有多年的英語教學經驗，但誰都沒在電視上教過課，更沒有編過系統的英語教材。這對我們確實是一個挑戰。經過了一番周折後，我們決定接受這個挑戰。

我們很快地成立了製作節目的小組。有意思的是，我們這幾個人中沒有一個是搞電視專業出身的。但我們都有一顆善良的，樂於助人之心。我們願意為北美的華人造福。通過我們的努力，讓每一位在北美的華人都有機會學說英語，擺脫語言的障礙，在北美發揮他們的特長。

我們決定打破以往的英語教學先教發音，再教辭彙，句子，課文，語法的規律，採用了小孩子學語言的方式，直接就教對話。讓人們學了就會說，學了就能用。我們的課程本著實用的原則，內容包括從在超級市場買東西到租房子，從看醫生到如何處理緊急情況。我們不只是講語言，還講北美的文化，人們的生活習慣，漢語用法和英語用法的不同之處等等。 在真人實景拍攝的節目中，我們沒有事先寫好腳本，而是“實話實說”，使對話更真實，實用價值更高。

讓我們感到欣慰的是"你好" 實用英語節目非常受歡迎。廣大觀眾紛紛給我們寫電子信，給電視台打電話，欲訂購書和錄影帶。許多觀眾給我們寫信說:“我們很想學英語，找了很多英語教材，這是我們找到的最好的一個。”在這裏我們非常感謝那些不斷給予我們支援的觀眾。雖然我們這個小組的每個成員都有工作，但我們走到一起，利用晚上和周末的時間製作了這套節目，並把授課內容編輯成書和光碟。這與觀眾朋友的鼓勵是分不開的。

我們把這本書獻給可貴的中國人民。希望通過學習一種新的語言和文化，在真誠，善良和忍讓中建立一種和諧的生活環境，使人們能夠生活得和平，美好，擁有真正的自由和幸福的未來。

如果你們在街上看到了我們，請別忘了停下來和我們打個招呼說一聲“Hello."

李仁德　丁慧

Contents 目錄

第一課 介紹你自己 Introducing Yourself

對話

A: Hello, how are you?
B: Fine, thank you. How are you?
A: I am fine. My name is Lee Ren De. What is your name?
B: My name is Ding Hui.
A: Nice to meet you.
B: Nice to meet you, too.

生詞

how 怎樣，怎麼

are 是
you 你
I 我
am 是
fine 好
my 我的
name 名字
is 是
what 什麼
your 你的
nice 好
to 常用於兩個動詞的中間，構成動詞不定式，在句子中沒有意思。
meet 見到
too 也

對話翻譯

A: 你好嗎？
B: 很好，謝謝。你好嗎？
A: 我很好，我叫李仁德。你叫什麼？
B: 我叫丁慧。
A: 很高興見到你。
B: (我)也很高興見到你。

對話解釋

英語的人稱

I 我，you 你，he 他，she 她

動詞 “是”

英語中的“是”與言語不同， 漢語只有一個是，而英語不同的人稱用不同的是。英語中的是有三種形式：是的變化隨著主語的人稱來變化

am are is

比如說，我是： I am， 你是： You are ， 他是：He is

is“是” 在英語中有時也表示一種狀態，是個動詞。

問題詞

用英語問問題時，常用問題詞。問題詞常放在一個句子的前邊。今天學的問題詞有 How 怎樣， What 什麼。

人稱的所有格

英語表達所有和漢語不一樣。 比如說，漢語中我的，英語用 my ，你的，英語用 your ，他的英語用 his/her ，所以，我們每個詞都要單獨記。

英語中的縮寫

有的英語為了說話方便起見，用縮寫形式

I am 變成 I´m

He is 變成 He´s
She is 變成 She´s
What is變成 What´s
I am fine. 可以說成 I´m fine.
He is fine. 可以說成 He´s fine.
She is fine. 可以說成 She´s fine.
What is your name? 可以說成 What´s your name?

練習

I. 把句子裏括號的詞翻成英文，再把句子完整地念一下:

Hello, how are (你) ?
Fine, thank you. (怎樣) are you?
(我) am fine.
How is (他) ? How is (她)?
(什麼) is (你的) name?
(我的) name is Ding Hui.
(他的) name is Tom. (她的) name is Mary.

II. 翻譯下面的句子：
很高興見到你。
你叫什麼名字？
我叫 Tom。
你叫什麼名字？
我叫 Mary。

很高興見到你。

III. 填空：(What, Nice, How, You, I)

1) Hello, how are __You__ ?

2) __I__ am fine.

3) __What__ is your name?

4) Hello, __How__ are you?

5) __Nice__ to meet you.

IV. 回答下面的問題：

1) Hello, how are you?

2) What is your name?

3) What is her name? (Mary)

第二課 這是什麼? What Is This?

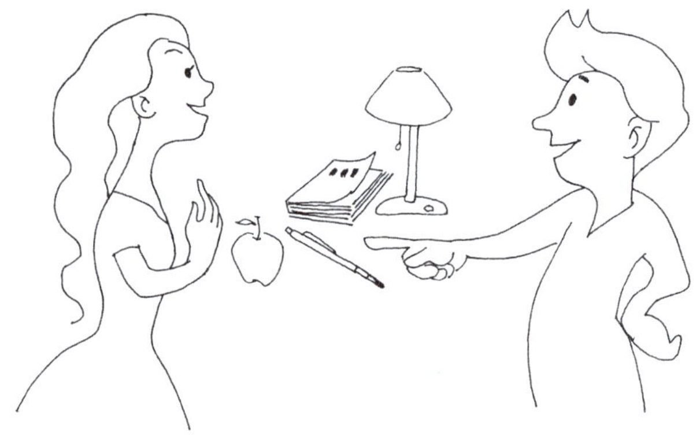

對話

A: What is this?
B: This is an apple.
A: What is that?
B: That is a pen.
A: What is this?
B: This is a lamp.
A: What is that?
B: That is a book.
A: What is this?
B: This is an envelope.

生詞

this 這

that 那 那个

apple 蘋果

pen 筆

lamp 燈

book 書

envelope 信封

對話翻譯

A: 這是什麼?

B: 這是一個蘋果。

A: 那是什麼?

B: 那是一隻筆。

A: 這是什麼?

B: 這是一盞燈。

A: 那是什麼?

B: 那是一本書。

A: 這是什麼?

B: 這是一個信封。

語法

敘述句

英語語法和漢語語法有很多相同的地方。"This is an apple" 和 "That is a pen" 用詞的順序和漢語的順序是一樣的，這兩個句子是敘述句。 敘述句用來陳述一件事實，包括肯定句和否定句。

英語的字母

英語共有二十六個字母，發音共分成兩個組，一組叫母音，在英語中只有5個母音，其他都是輔音。這些母音是 A, E, I, O, U. 剩下的字母都是輔音。 輔音字母不用單獨記，只要把母音字母記下來就可以了。所以，如果一個字是由母音開始的，前面一定要用 an 。為什麼用 an呢? 為了發音方便和好聽。 比如說，This is an apple. This is an envelope. “apple” 和 “envelope” 兩個詞的第一個字都是以母音開始 “apple” 的第一個字母是 a， “envelope” 的第一個字母是e。所以我們在這兩個字的前面要用an。 This is an apple. This is an envelope. a 和an 這兩個字都是 “一” 的意思。在英語中很少用量詞，所以翻譯的時候我們可以加上量詞。比如說量詞“個”，量詞“支”，等等。

一般疑問句

用來提出疑問的句子叫做疑問句。末尾用問號 “?”。把敘述句裏的動詞be 提到前面去，就變成了疑問句。一般疑問句，用 yes 或 no 來回答。比如：

Is that a pen?

那是一支筆嗎?

Yes, it is.

對，是。

Is this your pen?

這是你的筆嗎？

Yes, it is. Thank you.

對，是。謝謝。

Is that a book?

那是一本書嗎?

No, it isn´t. It is an envelope.

不，不是。那是一個信封。

Is this your lamp?

這是你的燈嗎？

No, it isn´t. This is your lamp.

不，不是。這是你的燈。

Oh, yes, thank you.

噢，對了，謝謝。

Is that my apple?

那是我的蘋果嗎?

No, it isn´t. It´s my apple.

不，不是。那是我的蘋果。

It 在這裡指已說過的東西，也有它和這個的意思。

not 的意思是不。is not ，是“不是”的意思。

isn´t 是 is not 的縮寫。

練習

I. 字母複習

1) 寫下英語的五個母音

_____ _____ _____ _____ _____

II. 用 a 和 an 填空

1) _____ pen

2) __a__ lamp 3) __an__ apple

4) __a__ book 5) __an__ envelope

III. 看圖答問題:

What is this?

1. 

2. ______________________________

3. ______________________________

4. ______________________________

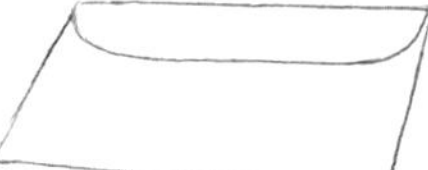

5. ______________________________

IV. 看圖答問題: Yes, it is. No, it isn´t

1. Is that a pen? ____________________

2. Is this an apple? ____________________

3. Is that an envelope? ____________

4. Is this a book? ____________________

5. Is that a lamp? ____________________

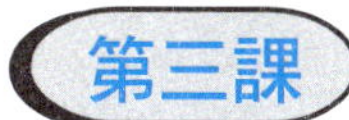 數目（一） Numbers (I)

對話（一）

A: Hello, how are you?
B: I'm fine, thank you.
A: What is your name?
B: My name is Ding Hui.
A: Nice to meet you.
B: Nice to meet you, too.
A: May I have your telephone number?
B: Sure. It is 540-872-6931. What is your phone number?
A: It's 864-2570. I will call you later.
B: OK, bye-bye.
A: Bye-bye.

生詞

May 可以
have 給我，取，拿
telephone 電話
number 號碼，數位
will 表示將來要做的事情
call 打電話
later 以後
sure 當然，沒問題

英語的數目

0 zero, 1 one, 2 two, 3 three, 4 four, 5 five, 6 six, 7 seven, 8 eight, 9 nine, 10 ten

對話翻譯

A: 你好嗎？
B: 我很好，謝謝。
A: 你叫什麼名字？
B: 我叫丁慧。
A: 很高興見到你。
B: 也很高興見到你。
A: 我能有你的電話號碼嗎？
B: 當然，是540-847-6931。你的電話號碼是什麼？
A: 是864-2570。我以後會打電話給你。

B: 好的，再見。
A: 再見。

對話 （二）

A: Hello, Ding Hui. How are you?
B: I´m fine. How are you?
A: Fine. Do you know Mary´s telephone number?
B: I´m sorry. I don´t know.
A: Do you know Tom´s telephone number?
B: Yes, it is 123-4567.
A: Thank you.
B: You are welcome.

生詞

know 知道，認識
Do you know 你知道嗎
Sorry 對不起
you´re welcome 不客氣

對話翻譯

A: 丁慧，你好嗎？
B: 我很好。你好嗎？
A: 很好。你知道瑪麗的電話號碼嗎？

B: 對不起，我不知道。
A: 你知道湯姆的電話號碼嗎？
B: 知道，是 123-4567 。
A: 謝謝。
B: 不客氣。

對話解釋

"Mary´s telephone number" 和 "Tom´s telephone number" 時 Mary´s， Tom´s 這裏的´s 表示英語的所有格。s 前邊有一個 ´ 省略號，意思是 “…的” 。

This is Mary´s pen. 這是瑪麗的筆。
That is Tom´s apple. 那是湯姆的蘋果。

練習

I. 把下面的名稱變成所有格

1) This is Mary´s pen. (Mary)
2) That is ________ apple. (Tom)
3) This is ________ telephone. (Lee)
4) That is __________ book. (Ding Hui)
5) This is __________ lamp. (Nancy)

II. 把下面的代詞變成所有格

1) What is your telephone number? (You)
2) _______ telephone number is 555-1234. (I)

3) What is _______ telephone number? (He)
4) _______ telephone number is 123-5545. (She)
5) Is this ________ pen? (You)

第四課 數目（二） Numbers (II)

對話

A: What are these?
B: These are apples.
A: What are those?
B: Those are pens.
A: What are these?
B: These are envelopes.
A: What are those?
B: Those are books.
A: Are these apples?
B: Yes, they are.
A: Are those apples, too?
B: No, they are not. They are pears.

生詞

these 這些

those 那些
they 他們
pear 梨

對話翻譯

A: 這些是什麼？
B: 這些是蘋果。
A: 那些是什麼？
B: 那些是筆。
A: 這些是什麼？
B: 這些是信封。
A: 那些是什麼？
B: 那些是書。
A: 這些是蘋果嗎？
B: 對，是。
A: 那些也是蘋果嗎？
B: 不，那些不是蘋果。那些是梨。

語法

單數和複數

在英語的名詞中有單數和複數的區別。幾個蘋果中的蘋果就不能只是一個 apple 了，而是多個 apples. 後面要加一個 "s", "s" 在這裏表示複數。這和漢語是不同的。漢語沒有單數和複數的區別，大家要記住。

如果我們用英語說一個以上的東西，這些，那些，就必須得用表示複數的代詞 these, those 。句子裏的動詞“是” 要用 are 。句子中的名詞要用複數。也就是名詞的後面要加 s 。

they 是他們的意思，可以指人也可以指物，也可以翻成這些、那些。

單數	複數	例子
apple	apples	These are apples.
pen	pens	These are pens.
book	books	These are books.
envelope	envelopes	These are envelopes.

練習

I. 把下面的單數名詞變成複數名詞

apple ______________

pen ________________

lamp ________________

envelope ____________

telephone ___________

II. 用複數回答問題: What are these?

____________________________ (lamp)

____________________________ (pen)

____________________________ (book)

__________________________________ (apple)

__________________________________ (envelope)

thirteen

fourteen

fifteen

sixteen

seventeen   eigheen

nineteen

twen

第五課 多少 How Many

對話

A: What are these?

B: These are flowers.

A: Are these your flowers?

B: Yes, they are.

A: How many flowers do you have?

B: I have 4 flowers. How many books do you have?

A: I have 2 books.

生詞

flower 花

how many 多少

have 有，只是用在我，你，我們，你們，他們後面

has 有，用在第三人稱單數 he 或 she 的後面

對話翻譯

A: 這些是什麼？
B: 這些是花。
A: 這些是你的花嗎？
B: 對，這些是(我的花)。
A: 你有多少朵花？
B: 我有四朵花。你有幾本書？
A: 我有兩本書。

對話解釋

How many flowers do you have? 這個句子的結構很常用，請把它寫下來。你可以把flowers這個詞拿掉，換上其他的名詞。

所謂助動詞就是幫助句子裏的動詞構成各種時態，語態，語氣，否定和疑問結構的詞。在句子裏沒有什麼意思， 也不能單獨作為語動詞。把敘述句變成問句和否定句時用 "do" 這個助動詞。 "do" 是個助動詞，第三人稱一般現在式單數的助動詞 do 就變成了 does 。比如：

How many lamps does she have?
She has 15 lamps.

How may telephones does he have?
He has 2 telephones.
How many pens do you have?
I have 7 pens.
How many books do they have?
They have 22 books.
I don´t have any apples.
We don´t have any books.
They don´t have a pen.
You don´t have a lamp.
He doesn´t have any apples.
She doesn´t have any flowers.
Mike doesn´t have his book.
Jennifer doesn´t have my pen.

在這些否定句裏，在have 的前面用助動詞do not have, 在第三人稱單數的句子裏用does not have. 你可能會問，為什麼不是does not has 呢？ 因為助動詞does在這裏就已經符合第三人稱條件了。don´t, 是do not 的縮寫，doesn´t 是does not 的縮寫。

練習

I. 用 have 或 has 填空

1. How many flowers do you ________?
2. Mary ________ 7 flowers.
3. I ________ 4 apples.
4. Tom ________ 2 lamps.

5. We don´t ___have___ any flowers.

II. 用完整的句子回答下面的問題

1. How many hats does he have? (4)
2. How many flowers do they have? (12)
3. Does Jennifer have any money? (no)
4. Do they have any apples? (yes)
5. Do we have any books? (no)

第六課 多少錢(一) How Much (I)

對話

A: Hello, how are you?
B: I'm fine.
A: Do you have any pens?
B: No, I don't. I'm sorry.
A: Oh, no problem. Do you have any lamps?
B: Yes, I do.
A: How much does a lamp cost?
B: A lamp costs 6 dollars and 45 cents.
A: Thank you.
B: You're welcome.

生詞

cost 價值

how much 多少錢
dollars 美元
cents 美分

對話翻譯

A: 喂，你好嗎？
B: 我很好。
A: 你有筆嗎？
B: 我沒有。對不起。
A: 哦，沒問題。你有燈嗎？
B: 對，我有。
A: 燈多少錢一台？
B: 六塊四毛五一台。
A: 謝謝。
B: 不客氣。

對話解釋

How much does this cost? 這個多少錢？這是標準的問價錢的句子。

Do you have any ... 你有沒有…？要問別人有沒有什麼東西，就用這個句型。

Do you have any pens? 你有筆嗎？

Do you have any lamps? 你有燈嗎？

練習

I. 用完整的句子回答下面的問題

1) How much does a lamp cost? ($4.30)
2) Does she have any pens? (No)
3) How much do pens cost? ($0.55)
4) Do they have any apples? (Yes)
5) How much do apples cost? ($0.20)

第七課 多少錢(二) How much(II)

對話

A: May I help you?
B: Yes, I want some bananas.
A: How many bananas do you want?
B: How much do bananas cost?
A: They cost 25 cents each.
B: Okay, I want 4 bananas.
A: That will be one dollar, please.
B: Here you are.
A: Thank you. Have a nice day.
B: You, too.

生詞

may 可以
help 幫助

banana 香蕉
each 每個，每人
Okay 好
here 這裏
nice 好，好的

對話翻譯

A: 我可以幫你嗎？
B: 可以，我想買香蕉。
A: 你想買幾根香蕉？
B: 香蕉怎麼賣？
A: 每根香蕉 25 分錢。
B: 好，我要四根。
A: 那一共一美元。
B: 給你錢。
A: 謝謝。祝你有個愉快的一天。
B: 你也一樣。

對話解釋

May I help you? 我可以幫你嗎？或者是我能為你做什麼？這是一個很有用的句子。如果你去商店買東西，售貨員一般都要和你說這句話。如果你不需要幫忙的話，就說 "No, thank you". 不用，謝謝。

Yes, I want some bananas. 好，我想要買點香蕉。“I want… ” “我想…”也是一個很有用的句型。 那麼我不想要怎麼說呢? "I don´t want ..." 我不想...如果你想做什麼，也用 "want"後面再加一個動詞。在英語裡如果句子裡有兩個動詞聯起來用的時候，一般在兩個動詞的中間加一個"to" 字，"to"在這裡不用翻譯出來。比如：

I want to go. 我想去。
I want to buy some bananas. 我想買點香蕉。

表達想要什麼或想做什麼很簡單。如果你想要什麼，用"I want" 後面加名詞就行了。如果你想要做什麼，"I want to" 後面加動詞就行了。

That will be one dollar. 一共一美元。will be 是“將是”的意思。 be 在這裡是“是“的意思。

Here you are. 當美國人給別人什麼東西的時候，經常說這句話。特別是用手遞給別人什麼東西的時候一般都說Here you are.

Have a nice day. 祝你有個愉快的一天。這是一句很好聽的話。一般都是在和別人分手時說的話。也是用另外一種說法說再見。

You, too. 直接翻譯出來就是，你也一樣的意思。英語說全了就是 You have a nice day, too.

練習

I. 用 "I want" 後面加名詞造句

1) I want an apple. (apple)
2) ________________________(banana)
3) ________________________(pens)
4) ________________________(lamp)
5) ________________________(envelopes)

II. 用 "I want" 後面加動詞造句

1) I want to go. (go)
2) ____________________(eat)
3) ____________________(sleep)
4) ____________________(buy)
5) ____________________(drink)

第八課 超級市場 The Supermarket

課文

A: This is a supermarket. Americans do all their shopping here. Today, we are going to teach you how to read the price for different food items and also the names of different kinds of food so you can go to the store and buy them yourself.
OK, let´s start here. This is an orange. Ding Hui, do you like oranges?
B: Yes, I do.
A: I do, too. Let´s see, oranges today are 2 for a dollar. Right, two oranges for a dollar. It´s a good deal.

This is the vegetable section. And this is a green pepper. Today, we have a sale. Sale usually means the price is lower for all times. They have hot price. Hot can mean temperature hot but in this case hot can mean very good. OK, today we have one dollar and 29 cents per pound for pepper.

These are bean sprouts. Bean sprouts cost one dollar and 29 cents per pound. There are carrots. Carrots are 79 cents per pound. There are green onions. Green onions cost 59 cents each. This is a cucumber. Cucumbers are 69 cents each. This is a ginger. This is a cauliflower. This is an eggplant. They are green beans.

This is the meat section. Americans buy all their meat in a packet. This is beef. This is pork. Supermarkets have club cards which can make the price lower. It is good to fill out the application and get yourself a card. It is free.

This is chicken. There are chicken wings. Supermarkets have sections like the vegetable section and meat section, but supermarkets also have aisles. This aisle has rice and juice. This is the diary section. This is milk. These are eggs. Eggs are sold by the dozen. These are cookies. This is a bread section. This is a loaf of bread. We hope you can go to a supermarket and buy what you need. If you have any questions you can ask the supermarket workers. They will be happy to help you.

生詞

Supermarket 超級市場
deal 交易，買賣
green 綠色
pepper 辣椒，胡椒
green pepper 青椒
bean 豆
sprout 苗
bean sprout 豆芽
carrot 胡蘿蔔
onion 蔥，洋蔥
green onions 青蔥
cucumber 黃瓜
ginger 薑
cauliflower 菜花
eggplant 茄子
bean 豆
green bean 四季豆
meat 肉
section 部門
beef 牛肉

free 免費，自由
net 純的，淨的
weight 重量
net weight 淨重
unit 單位, 單位的
unit price 單位價格
total 總計的(金額)，全部的
total price 總額
save 儲蓄，節約
aisle 過道，區域
rice 大米
juice 果汁
diary 奶製品
milk 牛奶
egg 雞蛋
cookie 餅乾
loaf 一條(麵包)，是量詞
bread 麵包
a loaf of bread 一條麵包

課文翻譯

A ： 這是超級市場，美國人在這裡買東西。今天我們要教你們如何讀不同食品種類的價錢，和不同食品的名稱，這樣你就能去商店自己買東西了。

好我們從這裡開始。這是桔子。丁慧，你喜歡桔子嗎?

B： 喜歡。

A： 我也喜歡。我們看一看。今天的桔子是兩個一美元。對，兩個一美元，很便宜。

這是蔬菜部。這是青椒。今天減價。減價的意思是價錢比較低。還有熱價錢。 hot 可以指溫度的熱，但在這裡hot的意思可以是非常好的。好，今天的青椒價錢是一美元 29 分一磅。

這些是豆芽。豆芽是一美元 29 分一磅。還有胡蘿蔔。胡蘿蔔 79 美分一磅。這裡有青蔥。青蔥的價格是 59 美分一把。這是黃瓜。黃瓜是 69 美分一個。這是薑，這是菜花。這是茄子，這是四季豆。

這是肉品部。美國人買肉是成包買。這是牛肉，這是豬肉。超級市場有會員證。拿會員證買東西能省錢。填個申請表，得到一張卡，對你很有好處。這是免費的。

這是雞，還有雞翅。超級市場分部門，像蔬菜部、肉部。但超級市場還有區域。這個區域有大米和果汁。這是奶製品部，這是牛奶。這些是雞蛋。雞蛋是以打賣的。這些是餅乾。這是麵包部。這是一條麵包。我們希望你能去超級市場買你需要的食品。如果你有問題，你可以問超級市場的工作人員。他們會很高興地幫助你的。

本課的目的是讓大家熟悉和了解超級市場的分佈和如何購買食品。句子都很簡單。請大家多記一些單詞，以便買東西時用。

練習

請將生詞和正確的詞義配合在一起

1) Bakery _______
2) Produce section _______
3) Sale ______
4) Expiration date ______
5) Dairy section ______

A) A special time where items in a store are cheaper.
B) Place where bread is made.
C) The date past which the food might be spoiled and can´t be sold.
D) Place where a store keeps its fruits and vegetables.
E) Place where a store keeps its milk and butter.

第九課 服裝店（一） Clothing Store(I)

對話

Clerk: May I help you?
Customer: Yes, I want to buy a T-shirt.
Clerk: What color do you like?
Customer: I like green.
Clerk: What size?
Customer: I wear an extra large.
Clerk: Do you like this one?
Customer: Yes, I do. How much is it?
Clerk: It is $12.00 dollars.

對話翻譯

售貨員：　我能幫你嗎？
顧客：　　是的，我想買件T恤衫。
售貨員：　你想要什麼顏色的？
顧客：　　我喜歡綠色的。

售貨員： 什麼號碼？
顧客： 我穿特大號。
售貨員： 你喜歡這件嗎？
顧客： 喜歡，多少錢？
售貨員： 12 塊錢。

生詞

buy 買
T-shirt T恤衫
color 顏色
like 喜歡
green 綠色
size 號碼
wear 穿
extra 特別
large 大

對話解釋

I want to buy a T-shirt。 如果一句話裡有兩個動詞，一般兩個動詞中間放一個 "to" 。這裡第一個動詞是want 想要，另外一個動詞是buy 買。比如，I want to eat dinner 我要吃飯。

我們來學習幾個有關穿著的詞:

dress 洋裝
skirt 裙子
pants 褲子
hat 帽子
shoes 鞋

dress 和 hat 是單數名詞。 pants 和 shoes 是複數。我們穿的鞋一般是兩隻，所以用複數。如果只說一隻鞋，那麼就用單數形式(shoe). 有意思的是英語的褲子這個字就只是複數。可能是因為褲子有兩條腿的原因吧。

說我喜歡什麼很容易，I like 後面加個名詞就行了。

I like apples.　我喜歡蘋果。
I like flowers.　我喜歡花。
I like books.　我喜歡書。

請大家注意，在這些句子裡的名詞都是複數。當我們講喜歡和不喜歡的時候，一般都用複數，複數代表一個整體。請大家記住這一點。

What do you like to do? 這裡的第一個 do 是助動詞，只起構成問句的作用，那麼第二個 do 是動詞，是做和幹的意思。英語中一詞多意的很多。這和漢語一樣。

練習脳

I. 看圖回答問題.

1) 

What is this? blue

This is a blue dress.

2) What is that? red

3) What is this? green

4) What are these? white

5) 

What are those? yellow

II. 用括號裏的詞回答下面的問題

1) What do you like? (apples)
2) What does John like? (green peppers)
3) What do they like to do? (play basketball)
4) What does she like to do? (read books)
5) What color do you like? (green)

第十課 服裝店（二） Clothing Store (II)

課文

This is Mike.
He is tall.
He wears a large shirt.
This is Mary.
She is short.
She wears a small shirt.
This is John.
He is fat.
He wears an extra large shirt.
This is Jennifer.
She is thin.
She wears a medium shirt.
This is my friend.
His name is Lee Ren De.
He is from America.

He is tall.
He likes to cook.
He has a blue shirt.
This is my friend.
Her name is Ding Hui.
She is from China.
She is short.
She likes to read books.
She has a red shirt.

生詞

Small 小號，縮寫是S
Medium 中號，縮寫是M
Large 大號，縮寫是L
Extra large 特大號，縮寫是XL
waist 腰，腰圍
inseam （褲管或衣袖的） 內縫
tall 高
short 矮
fat 胖
thin 瘦
friend 朋友

課文翻譯

這是麥克。

他高個子。
他穿一件大號的襯衫。
這是瑪麗。
她矮個子。
她穿一件小號的襯衫。
這是約翰。
他很胖。
他穿一件特大號的襯衫。
這是傑妮弗。
她很瘦。
她穿一件中號的襯衫。
這是我的朋友。
他叫李仁德。
他是美國人。
他個子高。
他喜歡燒飯。
他穿一件藍色的襯衫。
這是我的朋友。
她叫丁慧。
她是中國人。
她個子矮。
她喜歡讀書。
她穿一件紅色的襯衫。

課文解釋

我們講一下如何用英語表達衣服的號嗎。What size?

什麼尺寸? I wear an extra large. 我穿特大號。美國的襯衣分幾個號碼。這些號碼是:

Small　　小號，縮寫是S

Medium　　中 號，縮寫是M

Large　　大 號，縮寫是L

Extra large　特大號，縮寫是XL

矮個的人一般穿小號，又高又大的人一般穿大號或特大號。Extra 這個字的意思與very 差不多，有時也表示額外的，附加的。美國的褲子一般是以尺碼來定大小。一個尺碼來定你的腰寬，一個尺碼來定你的褲腿長度。美國人用英寸來量褲子。中國用尺。許多商店裡都有試衣間。在你買衣服之前你可以先試一下你挑選的衣服是否合適，然後再決定買不買。

練習

I. 閱讀問答

John is from America. He is tall. He wears extra large shirts. His shoes are red. His pants are green. He likes apples. John also likes to drink tea.

1) Where is John from?
2) What color are his shoes?
3) What does John like to do?
4) What size shirts does John wear?
5) Is John short?

II. 寫一段介紹你們家人的小短文

星期 Days of the Week

對話

A: What day is today?

B: Today is Friday.

A: Oh, really? Do you want to see a movie today?

B: Sorry, I am busy today.

A: Let´s go tomorrow.

B: Sure.

生詞

day 天，日

today 今天

Friday 星期五

really 是嗎

see 看
movie 電影
busy 忙
let´s 讓我們
go 走
tomorrow 明天
yesterday 昨天
this week 這周
next week 下周
everyday 每天

對話翻譯

A: 今天是星期幾？
B: 今天是星期五。
A: 噢，是嗎? 你今天想看電影嗎?
B: 對不起，我今天忙。
A: 那我們明天去吧。
B: 好哇。

對話解釋

What day is today? 今天是星期幾？What day 是指星期幾，不指日期。

Do you want to see a movie today? 你今天想看電影嗎? Do you want to 這個句型非常有用，在這

句話中我們在句子的後面有一個 today。在英語裡，表示時間的詞一般放在句子的後面。

Let´s go tomorrow. 我們明天去吧。 Let´s 後邊加動詞是建議大家在一起做什麼的意思。這是個很常用的表達方法。

語法

動詞的時態

在漢語中無論動作是什麼時候發生的，動詞形式基本上沒有什麼變化，例如他昨天去，他明天去，都用同一個字「去」來表示。而英語則不同。不同時間發生的動作要用不同形式的動詞表示。如: 他昨天洗襯衣了，He washed his shirt yesterday. 他明天洗襯衣。He will wash his shirt tomorrow. 這個句子裡的動詞 wash 發生了變化。句子中的動詞用來表示動作(情況)發生時間的各種形式稱為時態。 英語中有許多時態，一共有 16 個。大家一聽可能要嚇一跳，「這麼多呀! 」不過沒有關係，常用的只有五個時態。我們以後會慢慢講。今天我們先講一講一般現在時態。

一般現在時態

我們用這個時態表達經常做的事情，習慣做的事情或重複做的事情。They cook everyday. 這個句子就是一般現在時態，一般現在時態中的動詞基本不變。We cook everyday. 因為我們每天都得吃飯，所以我們每天就得燒飯，在這種情況下我們用一般現在時態。如果句中的主語是第三人稱 he or she或者是某個人的話，動詞的後面要加 s 。例如，He cooks everyday. 他每天燒飯。

動詞	現在一般時態
be	I am a student
	You are a student.
	He She is a student.
	We You are students.
have	They I You have 3 books. We They
	He She has 3 books.
study	I You We study English. They

練習

I. 請把下面的句子翻成漢語

1) I am busy today.

2) Do you want to see a movie today?

3) Sure.

4) I like Sundays.

5) I like Fridays.

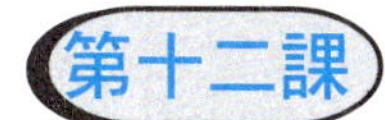

談時間　Telling Time

對話

A: Excuse me.

B: Yes?

A: Do you know what time it is?

B: Yes, it's two o'clock.

A: Thank you.

B: You're welcome.

A: What time is it?

B: It's 15 to 3 in the afternoon.

A: What time is it?

B: It is 7:30 in the morning.

A: What time is it?

B: It is 6 o'clock.

A: What time is it?

B: It is 20 past 10 at night.

生詞

Excuse 原諒，寬恕
Excuse me 對不起
time 時間
o´clock 整點
clock 時鐘
morning 早上
afternoon 下午
evening 晚上
past 過了
night 夜晚

對話翻譯

A: 對不起。
B: 什麼事？
A: 你知道幾點了嗎？
B: 知道，兩點了。
A: 謝謝。
B: 不客氣。
A: 幾點了？
B: 下午差十五分三點。
A: 幾點了？
B: 早晨七點三十分。
A: 幾點了？
B: 六點了。

A: 幾點了？
B: 晚間十點二十。

對話解釋

Excuse me 通常用來打斷別人說話，或者開始想跟別人說話的禮貌說法。Yes. 在這裡不是「是」的意思。是對別人的一個回答。可以翻成「什麼事」？ Do you know what time it is? 你知道現在是幾點了嗎? 問時間的基本句子是，What time is it? 幾點了? 在這個對話裡，我們用了比較禮貌的說法know 是知道的意思，「Do you know」你知道嗎? 「what time it is」意思是幾點了。如果你想問一個陌生人一個問題，這是一個最好的句子。注意Do you know 後面接的句子是敘述句，而不是問句。因為Do you know 已經是問題了。o´clock 是of the clock 的縮寫，意思是幾點鐘。用在整點的時間。把數字後面加一個o´clock 就表示幾點了。It´s 15 to 3 in the afternoon. 這裡的15 to 3指的是到3點還差15分鐘，如果說It´s 5 to 8 in the morning. 指的就是還差 5 分鐘就 8 點了，to 連接前後兩個數字，前面是分，後面是幾點。It´s 20 past 10. 的意思則是 10 點已經過了 20 分了，也就是 10 點 20 分的意思。Past 同樣連接兩個數字，前面是分，後面是幾點。

練習

I. 根據下面的時間回答問題

What time is it?

1)

2)

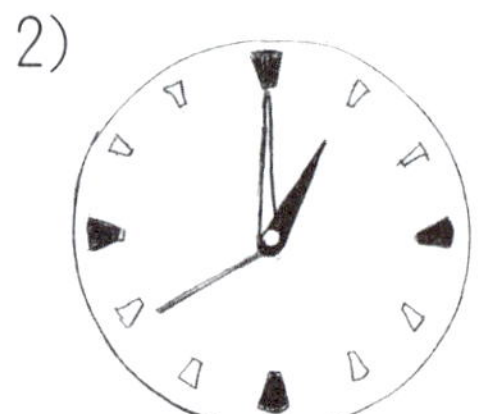

3)

4)

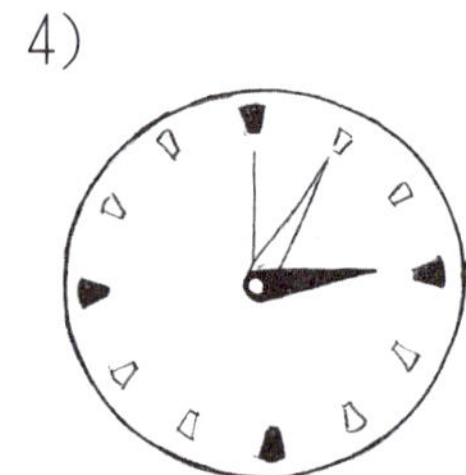

5)

II. 填空

1) (8:30) It is _______ past 8.
2) (3:45) It is ________ to 4.
3) (9:00) It is 9 __________.
4) (10:40) It is 20 ______ 11.
5) (12:05) It is 5 _______12.

第十三課 動詞 Verbs

對話（一）

A: Hello, how are you?

B: I´m fine. How are you?

A: Fine. What is your name?

B: My name is Lee Ren De. I work at the school.

A: Oh, really! I study English.

B: That´s great.

A: I read my English books everyday.

B: I write lessons everyday.

A: That´s interesting.

B: See you later.

A: Goodbye.

生詞

work 工作
study 學習
read 讀
write 寫
lessons 課程，教學
plan 計劃
lesson plan 教學計劃，教案
great 偉大的，了不起的，絕妙的
That´s great 那太好了
interesting 有意思的，有趣的

對話翻譯

A: 喂，你好嗎？
B: 我很好。你好嗎？
A: 很好。你叫什麼名字？
B: 我叫李仁德。我在學校工作。
A: 哦，是嗎！我學英語。
B: 那太好了。
A: 我每天都讀英語書。
B: 我每天寫教案。
A: 真有意思。
B: 回頭見。
A: 再見。

對話（二） 家庭生活

A: Hello, Ding Hui, Are you busy today?
B: Yes, I wash my clothes on Sundays.
A: I´m busy today, too.
B: Oh, really?
A: Yes, I cook dinner everyday.
B: That reminds me.
A: What?
B: I need to buy groceries.

生詞

wash 洗
clothes 衣服
cook 燒飯
need 需要，必須
remind 提醒
grocery 食品，菜

對話翻譯

A: 喂，丁慧，你今天忙嗎？
B: 對，我星期天洗衣服。
A: 我今天也忙。
B: 哦，是嗎？
A: 對， 我每天都燒晚飯。

B: 那倒提醒了我。
A: 什麼?
B: 我得買食品去。

對話解釋

That reminds me。那倒提醒了我,或者說你說的話提醒了我。這是一個比較常用的句子。最後一句話比較難。“I need to buy groceries.” need 是需要,必須的意思。buy 是買的意思。這個字我們以前學過。groceries 是grocery的複數形式。如果你需要做什麼 或 你必須得做什麼,在 need 後面加 to 再加動詞就行了。例子:

I need to wash my clothes.
He needs to buy groceries.
We need to study.

對話(三)娛樂

A: Finally, we have some free time.
B: Yes, what will we do?
A: We can watch TV.
B: I don´t want to watch TV.
A: Let´s play basketball.
B: I´m too short.
A: I want to ride my bicycle.

B: Okay, that´s fine. I just want to sleep.

生詞

finally 終於，最後
free 自由
free time 空閒時間
watch 看，觀察
play 玩，打(球)
basketball 籃球
too 太
Ride 騎(車)
bicycle 自行車
just 僅僅，就
sleep 睡覺

對話翻譯

A: 我們終於有點空閒時間了。
B: 是呀，我們做點什麼呢？
A: 我們可以看電視。
B: 我不想看電視。
A: 我們打籃球吧。
B: 我太矮了。
A: 我想騎自行車。
B: 好，那行啊。我就想睡覺。

對話解釋

free time 空閒時間，“Finally, we have some free time”我們終於有點自己的時間了。“I just want to sleep.” just want 就想，只想。我現在想做的事就是睡覺。

例子：
I just want to cook dinner.
He just wants to do grocery shopping.
Do you just want to sleep?

練習

I. 用括號裡的詞回答問題

1) What does Tom like to do? (watch TV)
2) What do we want to do on Sunday? (wash clothes)
3) When do they play basketball? (on Fridays)
4) What does Mary study? (English)
5) Who works on Saturdays? (Lee)

第十四課 在餐館裡(一) At the Restaurant (I)

對話 （一）

A: Excuse me, Ding Hui.
B: Yes, what do you want?
A: Do you know what time it is?
B: Yes, it is 6:30.
A: What do you want to do?
B: Let´s go to a restaurant.
A: Okay.

生詞

restaurant 餐館
okay 好吧

對話翻譯

A: 對不起，丁慧。
B: 啊，你想幹什麼？
A: 你知道幾點了嗎？
B: 六點半了。
A: 你想幹什麼？
B: 我們去餐館吧。
A: 好吧。

對話 （二）

Host: Hello, how are you today?
A: I´m fine.
B: I´m fine, thank you.
Host: How many people are in your party?
A: Two.
Host: Do you want smoking or non-smoking?
B: Non-smoking, please. We don´t smoke.
Host: Okay, please follow me.

生詞

people 人
party 同行者
in your party 這夥人
smoking 吸煙
non-smoking 不吸煙

table 桌子
chair 椅子
fork 叉子
knife 刀
spoon 勺
chopsticks 筷子
glass 玻璃杯
plate 盤子
bowl 碗
napkin 餐巾紙
menu 菜單
waiter 男招待
waitress 女招待
bill 賬單
check 賬單

對話翻譯

領位的： 喂，你們今天好嗎？
A: 我很好。
B: 我很好，謝謝。
領位的：你們一共幾個人？
A: 兩個。
領位的：你們想要吸煙的（座位）還是不吸煙的（座位）？
B: 不吸煙（座位）。我們不吸煙。
領位的： 好，請跟我來。

對話解釋

在美國，去餐館時，你一般不能想坐哪就坐哪。 進門的時候，門口會有一位領座的，英語叫 host男領位或 hostess女領位，他／她 會問你幾位，吸煙不吸煙。然後他／她會領你到給你的座位上去。How many people are in your party? in your party 可以理解為你們這些人。How many people are in your party? 你們一共有多少人? Please follow me.請跟我來。please 在這裡表示禮貌 。

練習

I. 把下面的句子譯成漢語

1) Let´s go to the restaurant.
2) We don´t smoke.
3) I need a fork.
4) What do you want to do?
5) How many menus do you want?

第十五課 在餐館裡(二) At the Restaurant (II)

對話

Waiter: Hello, my name is Mike. I will be your server this evening.

A: Hello.

B: Hello.

Waiter: Can I get you something to drink?

B: I want a coke, please.

A: Do you have tea?

Waiter : Yes, we do.

A: I want some tea, please.

Waiter : Okay.

Waiter: What do you want to eat?

B: I want the chicken sandwich.

A: I want the beef soup.

Waiter: Do you want anything else?

B: No, thank you. Please give us the check.
Waiter: Here you are.
A: Thank you. The food was delicious.

生詞

server 服務員
coke 可口可樂
tea 茶
chicken 雞
sandwich 三明治
beef 牛肉
soup 湯
delicious 好吃，可口
anything 東西
drinks 飲料
Sprite 雪碧
tea 茶
coffee 咖啡
milk 牛奶
water 水
pasta 意大利麵條
salad 沙拉，涼菜
cake 蛋糕
ice cream 冰淇淋
pie 餡餅，這種餡餅一般中間加水果
pudding 布丁

對話翻譯

男招待：我叫麥克，今天晚上我是你們的服務員。

A: 你好。

B: 你好。

男招待： 我可以給你們點什麼喝的嗎？

B: 我想要可口可樂。

A: 你有茶嗎？

B: 有。

A: 我想要茶。

男招待： 好。

男招待： 你們想吃點什麼？

B: 我想要雞肉三明治。

A: 我想要牛肉湯。

男招待：你們還想要點別的嗎？

B: 不要，謝謝。請把帳單給我。

男招待： 給你。

A: 謝謝。飯很好吃。

對話解釋

Can I get you something to drink? can 在這裡表示請求。can 的後面要用動詞的原形。Do you want anything else? anything 用於否定或疑問句裡，例如這句話就是疑問句。還有一個動詞「Need」需要，Need 也是一個很有用和很常用的詞。但是 want 和 need兩個詞並不很禮貌。 下面我們教你們一種比較禮貌想要什麼的說法。What would you like? 意思是你想要什麼? 這種說法在英語中很禮貌。I would like to drink some tea, please. 我想要喝茶。這也是非常禮貌的回答。I would like to 後面加動詞就是我想要做什麼的禮貌說法。I want 或I need 聽起來很生硬。

語法

一般將來時態

表示將要發生的事情，或以後要幹的事用一般將來時態。比如I will be your server this evening. will 在句子裡沒有意思,只是起語法作用。在will 後面的動詞要用動詞的原形。比如這句話裡的will be.

一般將來時態的構成：

主語＋will+動詞原型

動詞	肯定	否定	疑問
eat	I will eat an apple.	I will not eat an apple.	Will you eat an apple?

練習

I. 看圖答問題:

What would you like to eat?

1) 

2)  ______________________________

3) ______________________________ 

4)  ______________________________

5) ______________________________ 

II. 把下面的句子譯成漢語

1) Would you like to drink some tea?
2) I would like to watch TV.
3) They would like to eat some apples.
4) Would she like to eat?
5) We would like to dance.

第十六課 你做什麼工作? What Do You Do?

對話 (一)

A: Hello, how are you?
B: I´m fine. How are you?
A: I´m fine. What do you do?
B: I´m a teacher. I teach students.
A: I´m a student. I study English.
B: That´s interesting. Do you like to study English?
A: Yes, I do.

生詞

teacher 教師，老師
teach 教， 教課
student 學生
study 學習

對話翻譯

A: 喂，你好嗎？
B: 我很好。你好嗎？
A: 我很好。你做什麼工作？
B: 我是教師。我教學生。
A: 我是學生。我學英語。
B: 那很有意思。你喜歡學英語嗎？
A: 嗯，我喜歡。

對話解釋

What do you do? 這是標準的問別人職業的句子。準確的翻譯可以說是「你做什麼工作？」 或者說「你幹什麼工作？」 如果說你幹什麼呢，在英語中是另一個說法，為了不讓大家搞混，我們以後再教你們怎麼說你幹什麼呢。

英語中有些職業的名稱很容易學。比如 teacher 「教師」這個詞，teach是教的意思。後面加er. teacher 就變成教師了。 er 在這裡指人。例如：

teach - teacher　　work - worker （工人）

對話 （二）

A: Hello, Lee Ren De, how are you?
B: I´m fine. How are you?
A: I´m fine. How is your friend Linda?
B: Linda is okay.
A: What does she do?
B: She is a doctor.
A: Oh, really?
B: Yes, she helps sick people.
A: That´s interesting.

生詞

doctor 醫生
help 幫助
sick 生病的
people 人

對話翻譯

A: 喂， 李仁德，你好嗎？
B: 我很好，你好嗎？
A: 我很好。你的朋友麗達好嗎？
B: 麗達很好。
A: 她幹什麼工作。
B: 她是醫生。

A: 哦，是嗎？
B: 對，她幫助病人。
A: 那挺有意思的。

語法

第三人稱一般現在式單數

我們談某人的職業時，都用一般現在時態。陳述一件現在的事或經常發生的事，也用一般現在時態。如果句子的時態是一般現在時態，跟在第三人稱單數後面的動詞要變化。比如，She helps sick people. 或者What does she do? 或 What does he do? do字變成了does, 因為是第三人稱。 當你回答What does she do? 這個問題時，你得用is這個詞回答，後面加職業的名稱。 例如，She is a teacher.

一般現在式句子裡的第三人稱單數後面的動詞要變化。這種變化是動詞後面加「s」. 如果動詞結尾的字母是以s, sh, ch, o 後面要加 「es」. 如果動詞結尾的字母是以「y」結尾的，要變y 為 i 後面加es. 例如:

work - works, help - helps, like - likes
go - goes, wash - washes, teach - teaches,
carry - carries, fly - flies

He works in a school.
She washes clothes on Sundays.

Tom goes to school everyday.

Marry always carries a book.

下面介紹一些有關職業的名詞：

lawyer 律師

computer programmer 電腦程序師

baker 麵包師，糕點師

police 警察

manager 經理

engineer 工程師

driver 司機

secretary 秘書，書記

postal worker 郵局工作人員

construction worker 建築工人

custodian 清潔工

security guard 保安人員

journalist 記者

actor 演員

dancer 舞蹈演員

government worker 政府工作人員

練習

1. 用正確的 am, are, is 填空

1) I ________ a doctor.

2) He ________ a journalist.

3) They ________ construction workers.

4) ________ she a teacher?
5) ________ you an actor?

II. 用括號裡的詞回答下面的問題

1) What does she do? (student)
2) What do they do? (police officers)
3) What do you do? (teacher)
4) What does he do? (baker)
5) What does Mary do? (secretary)

第十七課 我的書在哪兒？Where Is My Book?

對話 (一)

A：Hi, Lee. What time is it?
B: It´s 8 o´clock.
A: Oh, no! I´m late for English class.
B: Don´t worry, Ding Hui.
A: Where is my English book?
B: I don´t know.
A: Here it is. It´s under the table.
B: Good. Now you can go.
A: See you later.
B: Good-bye.

生詞

hi 嗨
late 晚
for 介詞，表示目標、去向
late for （幹什麼）晚了
English 英語
class 課
worry 著急
don´t worry 別著急
under 在 ... 下
go 去

對話翻譯

A: 嗨， 李，幾點了？
B: 八點。
A: 哦，可不好了！我上英語課晚了。
B: 別著急，丁慧。
A：我的英語書在哪兒？
B: 我不知道。
A: 在這兒。在桌子底下。
B: 好，你可以走了。
A: 回頭見。
B: 再見。

對話解釋

Where is my English book? Where is .... ? 這是個很有用的句型。意思是 「…在哪裡？」

對話 （二）

A: Where is my book?
B: It is on the table.
A: Where is my book?
B: Your book is under the chair.
A: Where is my book?
B: It is next to the pen on the table.
A: Where is my book?
B: It is between the lamp and the flowers.
A: Where is my book?
B: It is beside the computer.
A: Where is my book?
B: It is in the drawer.
A: Where is my book?
B: It is near the telephone.

生詞

on 在 ...上
in 在 ...裡面

under 在 ...下
beside 在 ...邊上
next 下一個
next to 緊挨著
between 在兩者之間
chair 椅子
drawer 抽屜
near 靠近
telephone 電話機

對話翻譯

A: 我的書在哪？
B: 書在桌子上。
A: 我的書在哪？
B: 書在椅子下面。
A: 我的書在哪？
B: 書在桌子上挨著筆的地方。
A: 我的書在哪？
B: 書在燈和花之間。
A: 我的書在哪？
B: 書在電腦旁邊。
A: 我的書在哪？
B: 書在抽屜裡。
A: 我的書在哪？
B: 書在電話邊上。

對話解釋

It is on the table. It 在這裡指書。is 是動詞，在句子裡沒有什麼意思，on 在什麼上，on the table 在桌子上。整個句子是，你的書在桌子上。It is next to the pen on the table. 這句話裡有兩個介詞，分別表示兩個方位。next to the pen on the table 在桌子上挨著筆的地方。It is between the lamp and the flowers. between後面一般都有兩個東西或人。

語法

介詞

介詞一般用來表示名詞與動詞的關係，或者是名詞於名詞或代詞之間的關係。比如說在什麼時間、在什麼地方、靠什麼手段做事，介詞與動詞、名詞、形容詞常有比較固定的搭配構成詞組。

練習

1. 看圖用括號裡的詞填空 (on, next to, between, under, in)

1)

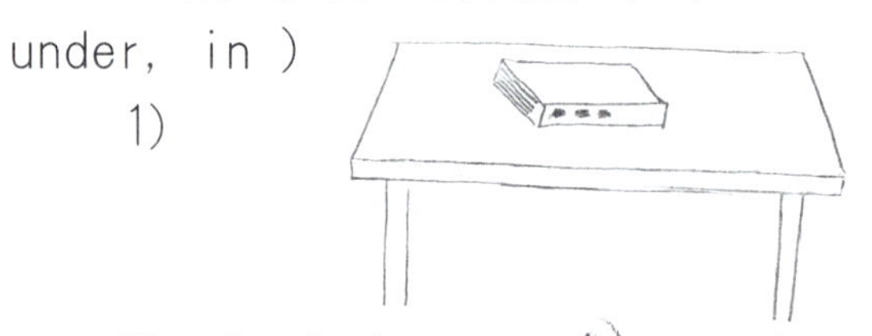

The book is ___________ the table.

2)

The telephone is between the book and the apple.

3)

The cat is ________ the chair.

4)

The lamp is __________ the telephone.

5)

The apple is _________ the backpack.

第十八課 找地方 Finding Places

對話 (一)

A: Hello Ding Hui, how are you?
B: I´m fine Lee. How are you?
A: Excellent. Where would you like to go today?
B: Today I´d like to go to the store. How about you?
A: I´d like to go to the library.
B: See you later.
A: Good-bye.

生詞

excellent 好極了
store 商店

library 圖書館

對話翻譯

A: 喂，丁慧，你好嗎？
B: 我很好李，你好嗎？
A: 好極了。你今天想去哪？
B: 今天我想去商店。你呢？
A: 我想去圖書館。
B: 回頭見。
A: 再見。

對話解釋

Where would you like to go today?
你今天想上哪兒去？這是一種很有禮貌的說法。有禮貌的回答是：
I would like to go to the store.
為方便起見，英語中的兩個字常縮寫成一個字。「I would」縮寫成 「I´d」。I´d like to go to the store. 我想去商店。How about you? 你呢？

下面我們看一下一些常用地點的名詞

school 學校
I´d like to go to the school.
bank 銀行

I´d like to go to the bank.

park 公園

I´d like to go to the park.

post office 郵局

I´d like to go to the post office.

ATM 取錢機

I´d like to go to the ATM.

movie theatre 電影院

I´d like to go to the movie theatre.

restaurant 餐館

I´d like to go to the restaurant

bus station 公共汽車站

I´d like to go to the bus station.

對話 (二)

A: Excuse me.

B: Yes?

A: Do you know where the post office is?

B: Yes, I do. The post office is next to the bank.

A: Thank you.

B: You´re welcome.

對話翻譯

A: 對不起。

B: 什麼事?

A: 你知道郵局在哪嗎？
B: 我知道，郵局緊挨著銀行。
A: 謝謝。
B: 不客氣。

練習

I. 把下面的兩個字縮寫

1) I would ____________
2) You would ___________
3) He would __________
4) She would ___________
5) They would ____________
6) We would ____________

II. 用 "I would," "you would," "he would," "she would," " they would, " "we would," 的縮寫形式回答下面的問題

1) Where would you like to go today?(library)
   I´d like to go to the library.
2) Where would he like to go today? (post office)
3) Where would they like to go today?
   (movie theatre)
4) Where would we like to go today? (park)
5) Where would she like to go today? (bank)

第十九課 左和右 Left and Right

對話

A: Excuse me.

B: Yes？

A: Where is the supermarket?

B: Go straight for 3 blocks. Turn left at the traffic light. Go 2 more blocks and it is on the right hand side of the street.

A: Thank you.

B: You´re welcome.

A: Have a nice day.

B: You, too. Good-bye.

生詞

left 左
right 右
turn 轉彎，轉動，翻轉，轉過身來 等
turn left 向左拐
turn right 向右拐
stop 停
go 走
go forward 往前開， 往前走
go backward 往後開，往後倒，往後走
go straight 往前走
back up 往後走，倒車
block 一條街（指連接在一起的一片建築物，兩條街中間夾的街）
traffic light 交通號誌燈
more 更多的
hand 手
side 邊
street 街道
right hand side 右手邊

對話翻譯

A: 對不起。
B: 什麼事？
A: 超級市場在哪？
B: 向前一直走三條街。在交通號誌燈那左拐，再走兩條街，超級市場就在街的右手邊。

A: 謝謝。
B: 不客氣。
A: 祝你有個愉快的一天
B: 你也一樣，再見。

對話解釋

一般的交通號誌燈有三種顏色的燈在上邊。這三種顏色分別是紅色、黃色和綠色。這三種顏色的功能分別是：Red means stop. 紅燈停。 Green means go. 綠燈行， Yellow means slow down. 黃燈減速，準備停。

再介紹幾個與路有關的新詞：

on the corner 位於街角
cross street 十字路口，過馬路
road 路
street 街道，馬路
avenue 大道
boulevard 大馬路

Road 路，Street 街道，馬路，Avenue 大道，Boulevard 大馬路這幾個字都有縮寫。 Road 的縮寫是 Rd. ，Street 的縮寫是 St. ，Avenue的縮寫是 Ave. ，Boulevard的縮寫是 Blvd. 。 在大城市裡，街道的名字有的是由號碼命名的，比如九街，十五街，在小城鎮裡街道都起了名，小城的主要街道一般都是直通市中心

的，許多商店都在市中心那。

練習

把下面的句子譯成漢語

1) The bank is between the supermarket and the movie theater.
2) Go backward.
3) The school is on Happy Avenue.
4) Turn left.
5) Go forward for 3 blocks.

第二十課 在路上 On the Road

課文

This is a stop sign.
When you see that, you must stop the car.
Where is the house?
The house is 2 blocks straight ahead, then turn right and go one more block.
It is on the left hand side of the street.
Here is a traffic light. It turns to yellow.
Slow down.
The 7 ELEVEN is next to the restaurant.
This is a gas station.
Regular gas is $1.49 for a gallon.
We are about to go on a really big high way - interstates high way.
This is a bridge.

Let´s take this main avenue.
Now we are going to back up or go backwards.
There is a parking meter.
LEFT LANE MUST TURN LEFT
Here is a bridge. We will go under the bridge.

生詞

Stop sign 停車的路牌
STOP 停 （路標）
go forward 向前走
turn right 向右轉
SPEED LIMIT 速度限制（路標）
parking sign 停車牌
PERMIT PARKING ONLY 許可證才能停（路標）
8AM - 5 PM 早上八點到下午五點（路標）
WEEKDAYS 平日 （星期一到星期五）（路標）
gas pump 加油泵
EXIT 出口 （路標）
interstates high way 州與州間的高速公路
DO NOT ENTER 不要進入 （路標）
ONE WAY 單行道 （路標）
a big intersection 一個大十字路口
PUBLIC PARKING 公共停車場 （路標）
parking lot 停車場
school cross walk 學校穿行區

15 MPH 每小時 15 英里 （路標）
bus stop 車站
DETOUR 彎路，迂路 （路標）

課文翻譯

這是一個停車的路牌。
你看到這個牌子就必須把車停下。
房子在哪裡?
那棟房子再向前走兩條街，向右拐，
再過一條街，在馬路的左邊。
這是一個交通號誌燈。
變成黃色了，減速。
7 Eleven 雜貨店緊挨著餐館。
這是個加油站。
普通的油每加崙一美元四毛九分。
我們就要到一條真正的大高速公路了—— 州與州之間的高速公路。
這是一座橋。
我們來走這條主街。
現在我們倒車。
這是停車計時器。
左線上的車一定要左拐。
這是一座橋，我們要走橋底下。

這課的目的是想讓大家瞭解如何看路標和如何找路。因為這課是我們開車在路上拍攝的，所以課文和生詞都是即時的，沒有經過周密思考。只做複習用。

練習

I. 把正確的路標填在句子的後面

Do Not Enter, Stop, Speed Limit, Exit, No Parking.

1) This sign tells you how fast you can drive. ________________
這個路標標明開車能開多快。

2) This sign means you must stop your car before you can drive on. ______________
這個路標標明你必須先停車才能再繼續往前開。

3) This sign means you cannot enter this road. ____________________
這個路標標明你不能開進這條路。

4) This sign states that you cannot park your car in that area. __________________
這個路標標明你不能在那個區域停車。

5) This sign labels a road you can use to get off a larger highway. ____________
這個路標指示你能利用某條路開下大型高速公路。

第二十一課 填申請表 Filling out an Application

對話

A: Hello Ding Hui, what is that?
B: This is an application.
A: What application?
B: I want to have a driver´s license. This is a driver´s license application.
A: That´s great.
B: Can you help me, please?
A: Sure.
B: What does this mean?

生詞

fill out 填(表)
application 申請表

driver 司機
license 執照
driver´s license 駕駛執照
mean 意思

對話翻譯

A: 喂，丁慧，那是什麼？
B: 這是一分申請表。
A: 什麼申請表？
B: 我想要一個駕駛執照。這是駕駛執照的申請表。
A: 那好啊。
B: 你能幫我嗎？
A: 當然能。
B: 這是什麼意思?

對話解釋

"Can you help me, please?" 和 "What does this mean?" 這兩個問題在日常生活中很常用。如果你需要誰幫忙，只要說 "Can you help me, please?" 別人就會來幫忙。你不知道什麼字或什麼話是什麼意思的時候，就對講英語的人問 "What does this mean?" 他們就會告訴你。

在申請表上經常要回答的內容有：

Social Security Number 社會安全號，有時也可以縮寫成SSN。社會安全號是九位數字000-39-4521。Gender 性別，性別只有兩種：Male 男，Female 女，寫對性別很重要。如果把男的寫成女的，女的寫成男的就有意思了。特別是美國人不能從我們的名字裡辨別出來是男還是女。

Date of birth 出生年月日。"date of birth" 一般要按照這個順序表示 "mm/dd/year" ，mm 代表月，dd代表日，最後是年year。這和漢語的順序不一樣。比如某人是1972年5月6日出生的，應寫成05／06／1972。

Daytime telephone number 白天的電話號碼， 有時表上也會問工作和家裡的電話，work number 工作電話， home number 家裡電話。 Last name 姓， First name 名，中國人名字的順序和美國人正好相反。美國人把名放在前面，把姓放在後面，而我們中國人把姓放在前面，把名放在後面。 Middle name 中間的名字，Middle initial 是中間名字的第一個字母大寫加上句點，例如中間名為Jason，Middle initial 就是J.，中國人一般並沒有Middle name。Maiden name 婚前姓氏，美國女性一般在結婚後都會改從夫姓，這個Maiden name 就是指結婚前的本姓。在填申請表的時候，如果某一欄目並沒有任何資料可以填，通常會填上N/A(not applicable)。

Residence 住宅， Home address 家庭住址，City 城市，Town 城鎮，State 州，Zip Code 郵政編碼，這就是美國人寫地址的順序，也和中國人相反。請大家注意。

我們介紹一下一年裡的十二個月

month 月
January 一月
February 二月
March 三月
April 四月
May 五月
June 六月
July 七月
August 八月
September 九月
October 十月
November 十一月
December 十二月

練習

I. 填下面的申請表

Last Name: ______________________

First Name: ______________________

Middle Initial: ______________________________

Maiden Name: ___________________________________

Date of Birth (mm/dd/yr):_____________________

Gender: Male or Female

Daytime Telephone Number: ____________________

Address:

Street City or Town State Zip Code

Are you a U.S. citizen?_______________________

What do you do? _______________________________

What is your employer's name(雇主的姓名), address, and telephone number?

____

____

第二十二課 你上哪去？ Where Are You Going?

對話

A: Hello, Lee Ren De. Where are you going?

B: I´m going to school.

A: Why?

B: I study Chinese everyday.

A: That´s interesting.

B: Where are you going?

A: I´m going downtown.

B: Why?

A: I want to buy some gifts for my friends.

B: Okay, see you later.

A: Good-bye.

生詞

school 學校

downtown 市中心
Gift 禮物

對話翻譯

A: 喂，李仁德，你去哪？
B: 我去學校。
A: 幹什麼去？
B: 我每天學漢語。
A: 那真有意思。
B: 你去哪？
A: 我去城裡。
B: 幹什麼去？
A: 我想給我的朋友買些禮物。
B: 好哇，回頭見。
A: 再見。

語法

現在進行時態

現在正在做的事情，我們把這個時態叫做現在進行時態。現在進行時態的構成是動詞be 加上另一個動詞，這個動詞後面加ing，這樣的動詞叫分詞。我們以前學過be這個詞。在用be這個詞的時候，我們知道要根據句子前面的主語變化。

現在進行時態的構成：

主語＋ be ＋ 動詞＋ ing

肯定	否定
I´m going to school.	I am not going to school.
You are going to school.	You are not going to school.
He She is going to school	He She is not going to school.
We You are going to school. They	We You are not going to school. They

一般現在時態和現在進行時態兩個時態的比較：

一般現在時態，是指經常發生的事情。現在進行時態是指現在正在發生的事情。比如 I study Chinese. 我學中文。如果誰說 I study 或者 you study 這就是說他們常做這件事情，也許他們在學校上一門課。 I´m studying Chinese 。我在學中文呢。如果誰說 「I´m studying」或 「you´re studying」就是說這個人在我們說話的時候手裡有一本書，他也許是在看書或是在做作業。

例如：

B：Hey Ding Hui. Where are you going?

A：I´m going downtown

B：What are you doing?

A: I´m studying English.

用不同的地點來練習一下

He´s going to the library.
You´re going to work.
I´m going home.
We´re going to the post office.
They are going to the doctor´s office.
She´s going to the hospital.
I´m going to the train station.
Mary´s going to the hotel.

下面我們介紹一些有關地點的生詞

library 圖書館
work 工作
home 家
post office 郵局
doctor´s office 醫生辦公室
hospital 醫院
train station 火車站
hotel 旅館

例子：

A: What are you doing?
B: I´m reading a book.
A: What is he doing?
B: He is writing a letter.
A: What are they doing?
B: They are playing basketball.

A: What are we doing?
B: We are studying English.

例子翻譯
A: 你幹什麼呢？
B: 我讀書呢。
A: 他幹什麼呢？
B: 他寫信呢。
A: 他們幹什麼呢？
B: 他們打籃球呢。
A: 我們幹什麼呢？
B: 我們學英語呢。

練習

I. 把下面的句子變成現在進行時態
1) I go downtown.
2) They study English.
3) We play basketball.
4) I eat pizza.
5) She drinks tea.
6) Tom reads a book.
7) You write an application.
8) My friend sleeps.

第二十三課 公共交通 Public Transportation

對話（一）

A: Where are you going?

B: I want to go downtown.

A: You need the number 12 bus.

B: Oh, really?

A: Yes. The fare costs $1.10. Do you have money?

B: Yes I do.

A: Do you have exact change?

B: I´m okay. Here is a dollar and here is a dime.

A: That´s great.

B: What time does the bus come?

A: The bus comes at 1 o´clock.

B: That´s in 10 minutes. I´m going to the bus stop now.

A: See you later.
B: Good-bye and thank you.

生詞

number 12 bus 十二路公共汽車
fare 車費
exact 正好
change 零錢
come 來
bus stop 公共汽車站

對話翻譯

A: 你去哪兒？
B: 我想進城。
A: 你需要乘 12 路公共汽車。
B: 哦，是嗎？
A: 是，車票價錢是一塊一，你有錢嗎？
B: 有。
A: 你有正好的零錢嗎？
B: 有。這是一塊錢，這是一毛錢。
A: 那太好了。
B: 公共汽車什麼時間來？
A: 一點來。
B: 那十分鐘之內就來了。我現在就去公共汽車站。

A: 回頭見。

B: 再見，謝謝。

對話解釋

Number 12 bus 十二路公共汽車。公車的名稱在各個城市都不同。你可以從公車站或加油站拿到免費的汽車路線圖。公車路線圖可以告訴你乘什麼車去哪裡。「fare」車費，不同的城市，車費也不同，你得問司機票價是多少錢。「What time does the bus come?」公共汽車什麼時間來？在美國，公共汽車和火車一樣也有個時間表。公車一般都是按點到站。時間表一般都貼在公車站的立柱上或者是汽車亭裡。

對話（二）

A: Hello.

B: Hello, where would you like to go?

A: I´d like to go to the Blue Hotel, please.

B: I don´t know where that is.

A: It is on the corner of 23rd street and Park Avenue.

B: Okay, let´s go.

A: How much is the fare?

B: It is $8.50.

A: Here is 10 dollars. Keep the change.

B: Thank you.

A: Good-bye.

生詞

keep 保留
Keep the change 把零錢留下

對話翻譯

A: 你好。
B: 你好，你想去哪兒？
A: 我想去藍色旅館。
B: 我不知道藍色旅館在哪？
A: 在二十三街和公園街的拐角處。
B: 好，我們走吧。
A: 車費多少錢？
B: 八塊伍毛。
A: 這是十元錢。零錢留下吧。
B: 謝謝。
A: 再見。

對話解釋

Keep the change. 這句話在你給服務人員錢的時候很常用。在美國給服務人員小費是個習慣。這些服務行業的人員包括餐館的招待員，理髮店的理髮員，旅館為你提行李的服務員，和出租車司機等。小費的數量一般是花錢總數的 15% 和 20% 。所以如果出租車的費用是 $8.50，你給 $10 就可以了，如果你的理髮費是 $10 呢，你就交 $12。如果你的飯錢是 $16，你給 $20 就比較合適。給餐館的服務員小費很重要，因為這些人掙的工資很低，全靠小費生活了。

對話（三）

A: Excuse me.
B: Yes?
A: What line is this?
B: This is the green line. Where do you want to go?
A: I want to go to the Chinatown station.
B: No problem. This is the right line.
A: Thank you.
B: You're welcome.

生詞

token 投幣
fare card 車票
line 鐵軌，路線
station 車站
Chinatown 中國城，唐人街
Chinatown station 中國城車站
right 對的，正確

right line 對的路線

對話翻譯

A: 對不起。
B: 什麼事？
A: 這是什麼線？
B: 這是綠線。你想去哪？
A: 我想去中國城車站。
B: 沒問題。這條線是對的。
A: 謝謝。
B: 不客氣。

對話解釋

在美國，地鐵系統各個城市都不同。紐約市的地鐵乘一次的票價無論到哪裡都一樣。那兒的地鐵票叫「tokens」. 在華盛頓，地鐵票叫 「fare card」。票價根據你乘車的遠近而定，越遠就越貴。「line」有的時候也叫「track」，這兩個字都是指火車走的鐵軌，許多城市地鐵不同線路都用顏色來命名，比如紅線，藍線等。

練習

用括號裡的動詞回答問題

1. What are you doing? (write letters)

2. What is he doing? (return a book)
3. What are they doing? (make phone calls)
4. What is Mary doing? (meditate)
5. What is Lee doing? (buy some stamps)

第二十四課 做不同的事 Doing Different Things

對話(一)

A: Hello Ding Hui. Where are you going?
B: I´m going to the library.
A: Why?
B: I want to return a book.
A: See you later.
B: Good-bye.

生詞

library 圖書館
return 歸還
return a book 歸還一本書

對話翻譯

A: 喂，丁慧，你去哪兒？
B: 我去圖書館。
A: 幹什麼去？
B: 我想還本書。
A: 回頭見。
B: 再見。

對話(二)

A: Hello Lee Ren De. What are you doing?
B: I´m reading a book.
A: What book is it?
B: It is a novel. I like to read novels.
A: I like to read novels, too.

生詞

novel 小說

對話翻譯

A: 喂，李仁德，你幹什麼呢？
B: 我讀書呢。
A: 什麼書？
B: 是本小說。我喜歡讀小說。
A: 我也喜歡讀小說。

對話解釋

在談話的時候李仁德正在看書，所以要用現在進行時態。這句話裡我們也談到了喜歡。I´m reading a book. 是一件正在發生的事。I like to read novels. 只是說喜歡和愛好，並不是在做一件事情，所以就用一般現在時態。

對話（三）

A: Hello Ding Hui. Where are you going?
B: I´m going to the post office.
A: Why?
B: I want to buy some stamps.
A: See you later.
B: Good-bye.

生詞

stamp 郵票

對話翻譯

A: 喂，丁慧，你去哪兒？
B: 我去郵局。
A: 幹什麼去？
B: 我想買郵票。

A: 回頭見。

B: 再見。

對話解釋

stamp是指一張郵票。如果你想買幾張郵票，你就得用「stamps」美國的郵局賣郵票是以大張為單位，一般一大張郵票上面有20個郵票， 叫做a book of stamps，一連郵票。

對話 （四）

A: Hello Lee Ren De. What are you doing?

B: I´m writing a letter.

A: That´s interesting.

B: I like to write letters.

A: I don´t like to write letters. I make phone calls.

生詞

letter 信， 字母

write 寫

phone telephone 的簡寫，電話

call 電話

make phone calls 打電話

對話翻譯

A: 喂，李仁德，你幹什麼呢？
B: 我寫信呢。
A: 真有意思。
B: 我喜歡寫信。
A: 我不喜歡寫信。我打電話。

對話解釋

李仁德正在寫信。所以這裡也要用現在進行時態。letter 是信的意思。write 這個字是寫的意思。大家注意writing這個字的拼寫。write 是以e 結尾的，那麼後面加ing 的時候就得把 e 去掉。這是動詞變成分詞的規律。我們把動詞後面加的ing 的詞叫做分詞。phone 是telephone 的簡寫，電話的意思， call 也是電話的意思，那麼make phone calls 就是打電話。

對話（五）

B: Hello Ding Hui. Where are you going?
A: I´m going to the park.
B: Why?
A: I want to meditate.
B: See you later.
A: Good-bye.

生詞

meditate 打坐, 深思, 冥想

對話翻譯

A: 喂，丁慧，你去哪兒？
B: 我去公園。
A: 幹甚麼去？
B: 我想打坐。
A: 回頭見。
B: 再見。

對話 （六）

A: Hello Lee Ren De. What are you doing?
B: I´m meditating.
A: Oh, I´m sorry.
B: That´s OK. I like to meditate.
B: I like to meditate, too.

對話翻譯

A: 喂，李仁德，你幹什麼呢？
B: 我冥想呢。
A: 哦，對不起。
B: 沒關係。我喜歡冥想。

A: 我也喜歡冥想。

對話解釋

A為什麼說I´m sorry呢，因為人在meditate的時候需要安靜，B正在打坐，A打擾他了，所以A得說對不起。That´s OK 是沒關係的意思。

練習

I. 閱讀下面的短文回答問題

Mary likes to buy clothes. Every Saturday she goes to the clothing store. The clothing store is at downtown. Mary takes the number 8 bus. The bus costs $1.50 each way. The bus comes to the stop exactly at 8:30 in the morning. Mary always goes to the bus stop at 8:20 in the morning. She doesn´t want to be late.

1) What does Mary like to do?
2) When does she go to the clothing store?
3) Where is the clothing store?
4) How much is the bus fare?
5) What time does the bus come to the bus stop?

II. 在這裡我鼓勵你用一天的時間，和你的會講英語的朋友或親戚出去瞭解一下你居住的城市。你最好乘汽車和地鐵，或乘出租車去看個節目。你的朋友或親戚只是在你需要的時候幫助你一下，你應該自己大膽地講英語別怕出錯。你如果對你周圍的環境有一個大概的瞭解，你的生活就能輕鬆一點。

第二十五課 天氣 Weather

對話 (一)

A: Good morning.
B: Good morning. How are you?
A: I´m fine. And you?
B: I´m fine. What´s the weather today?
A: Today is sunny and warm.
B: That´s great.
A: Maybe.
B: Why maybe?
A: Our farmers need rain.
B: That´s true.

生詞

Good morning 早上好
Good afternoon 下午好
Good evening 晚上好
weather 天氣
sunny 晴朗的
warm 溫暖的
farmer 農民
rain 雨
true 真的

對話翻譯

A: 早上好。
B: 早上好。你好嗎?
A: 很好,你呢?
B: 很好。今天天氣怎麼樣?
A: 今天天氣晴朗而且暖和。
B: 太好了。
A: 也許是吧。
B: 為什麼也許是呢?
A: 農民需要雨呀。
B: 那倒是真的。

介紹一些有關大自然的詞和句子

sunny 晴朗
cloudy 多雲
rainy 下雨的
windy 颳風
snowy 下雪
The sun is yellow. 太陽是黃色的。
moon 月亮
The moon is full. 月亮是滿月。
cloud 雲
The cloud is white. 雲是白色的。
sky 天
The sky is blue. 天是藍色的。
wind 風
The wind is cool. 風有些涼。
snow 雪
The snow is white. 雪是白的。

sun, cloud, rain, wind, and snow 都是名詞。那麼形容天氣要用形容詞。我們把這些名詞後面加上「y」就變成形容詞了。那麼sun 就變成了 sunny 晴朗，cloud 就變成了cloudy 多雲，rain 變成了rainy 下雨的， wind 變成了windy 颳風，snow 變成了snowy 下雪的。

表達溫度的詞

hot 熱

warm 暖和
cool 涼，涼爽
cold 冷

對話 (二)

A: Good morning.
B: Good morning. How are you?
A: I´m fine. And you?
B: I´m fine. What´s the weather today?
A: Today is windy and cool.

對話翻譯

A: 早上好。
B: 早上好。你好嗎？
A: 很好，你呢？
B: 很好。今天天氣怎麼樣？
A: 今天颳風還有點冷。

對話 (三)

A: Good morning.
B: Good morning. How are you?
A: I´m fine. And you?
B: I´m fine. What´s the weather today?
A: Today is snowy and cold.

對話翻譯

A: 早上好。
B: 早上好。你好嗎？
A: 很好，你呢？
B: 很好。今天天氣怎麼樣？
A: 今天又下雪又冷。

對話 （四）

A: Good morning.
B: Good morning. How are you?
A: I´m fine. And you?
B: I´m fine. What´s the weather today?
A: Today is cloudy and rainy.

對話翻譯

A: 早上好。
B: 早上好。你好嗎？
A: 很好，你呢？
B: 很好。今天天氣怎麼樣？
A: 今天陰雨綿綿。

練習

I. 看圖用括號裡的詞造句（Sunny, Cloudy, Windy, Rainy, Snowy）

1

____

2) ______________________________

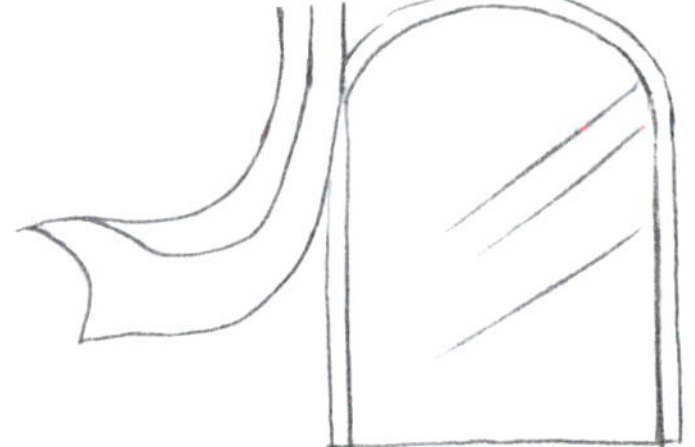

____

4) ______________________________

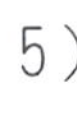

5）

____

第二十六課 你感覺如何？ How Do You Feel?

有關身體的詞和句子

This is my head. (Head) 這是我的頭。
These are my eyes. (Eyes) 這是我的眼睛。
These are my ears. (Ears) 這是我的耳朵。
This is my nose. (Nose) 這是我的鼻子。
This is my mouth. (Mouth) 這是我的嘴。
These are my arms. (Arms) 這是我的胳膊。
These are my hands. (Hands) 這是我的手。
These are my fingers. (Fingers) 這是我的手指。
I have one, two, three, four, five, six, seven, eight, nine, ten fingers.

我有一、二、三、四、五、六、七、八 、九、十，十隻手指。

These are my shoulders. (Shoulders) 這是我的肩膀。

This is my chest. (Chest) 這是我的胸。

This is my stomach. (Stomach) 這是我的胃。

These are my legs. (Legs) 這是我的腿。

These are my feet. (Feet) 這是我的腳。

This is a foot. (Foot) 這是一隻腳。

These are my knees. (Knees) 這是我的膝蓋。

These are my toes. (Toes) 這是我的腳趾。

I have ten toes. 我有十個腳趾。

兒歌

Head, shoulders, knees, and toes - knees, and toes.
Head, shoulders, knees, and toes - knees, and toes.
Eyes, and ears, and mouth, and nose.
Head, shoulders, knees, and toes - knees, and toes.

對話（一）

A: Hello, Lee Ren De. You look good.

B: Really? Thank you.

A: How do you feel?

B: I´m happy.

A: That´s great.
B: Yes, today is a beautiful day.

生詞

look 看上去
happy 高興，幸福，快樂
I´m happy 我高興
beautiful 美麗，漂亮

對話翻譯

A: 你好，李仁德，你看上去很好。
B: 是嗎？謝謝。
A: 你感覺怎麼樣？
B: 我很高興。
A: 那太好了。
B: 今天是美麗的一天。

對話解釋

How do you feel? 你感覺如何?「feel」是從「feelings」這個詞來的。這個問話比「How are you?」更明確一點。「How are you?」也是問你身體怎麼樣，但是只是個客氣的話。你並不一定真想知道這個人的身體怎麼樣。回答也是很隨便。當你說「How do you feel?」時，你是真想知道對方的感覺如何。

有關感覺的詞

sad 難過，憂傷，悲傷
I feel sad. 我很難過。
calm 鎮定的，無憂慮的
I feel calm. 我很鎮定。
worried 著急的
I feel worried. 我很著急。
sick 病，生病
I feel sick. 我覺得我有病了，我生病了。

我們可以用兩種不同的方法回答「How do you feel?」這個問題。 一種方法是「I´m happy.」 或「I´m sick.」 另一種方法是 「I feel happy.」 或「I feel sick.」

對話 （二）

A: Hello, Lee Ren De. You look terrible.
B: I know.
A: How do you feel?
B: I feel sick.
A: Oh, really?
B: Yes, I have a headache.
A: I´m sorry.
B: Thank you. I need to sleep.

生詞

terrible 可怕的，很壞的
headache 頭疼
ache 疼

對話翻譯

A: 你好，李仁德，你看上去很不好。
B: 我知道。
A: 你感覺怎麼樣？
B: 我不舒服。
A: 是嗎？
B: 對，我頭疼。
A: 對不起。
B: 謝謝，我得睡覺去。

語法

複合詞

「head」是頭的意思。「ache」 是疼的意思。把這兩個字放在一起「headache」就是頭疼的意思。兩個詞加在一起構成一個詞這叫複合詞。

例如：stomachache 胃疼， earache 耳朵疼，
toothache 牙疼

對話 （三）

A: Hello, Lee Ren De. You look terrible.
B: I know.
A: How do you feel?
B: I feel sick.
A: Oh really?
B: Yes, I have a stomachache.
A: I´m sorry.
B: Thank you. I need to sleep.

生詞

stomach 胃，肚子
ache 疼
stomachache 胃疼或肚子疼
hurt 疼
earache 耳朵疼
toothache 牙疼

例句

I have a toothache 我牙疼
My arm hurts 我胳膊疼
My head hurts 我頭疼
My knee hurts 我膝蓋疼
My stomach hurts 我胃疼
My finger hurts 我手指疼

對話翻譯

A: 你好，李仁德，你看上去很不好。
B: 我知道。
A: 你感覺怎麼樣？
B: 我不舒服。
A: 是嗎？
B: 對，我胃疼。
A: 對不起。
B: 謝謝，我得睡覺去。

練習

I. 把下面的句子譯成英文，用（feel）
1） 瑪麗感到很高興。
2） 我感覺生病了。
3） 湯姆很著急。
4） 我們感到悲傷。
5） 她感到很鎮靜。

II. 把下面的句子譯成漢語
1） I have a stomachache.
2） My knee hurts.
3） He has an earache.
4） Her hand hurts.
5） Tom has a headache.

第二十七課 預約 Making an Appointment

對話

A: This is the doctor's office. How may I help you?

B: Hello, my name is Ding Hui. I feel sick.

A: What's the matter?

B: I have a stomachache.

A: Do you want to make an appointment?

B: Yes, I do.

A: Can you come in this afternoon at 4 o'clock?

B: Sure. Thank you.

A: You're welcome.

B: Good-bye.

A: Good-bye. See you at 4 o'clock.

生詞

help 幫助
matter 事情，問題，事務
appointment 預定，約會
come 來

對話翻譯

A: 這裡是醫生診所，我能怎麼幫你？
B: 你好，我叫丁慧，我不舒服。
A: 怎麼了？
B: 我胃疼。
A: 你想預約嗎？
B: 想。
A: 今天下午四點鐘來可以嗎？
B: 可以， 謝謝。
A: 不客氣。
B: 再見。
A: 再見。四點見。

對話解釋

醫生這個職業分不同的科，比如說兒科、內科、外科等等。上次課我們講了怎麼說牙疼，「I have a toothache.」。如果你真的牙疼或其他的牙病。你要和牙醫預約，牙醫是「dentist」。

對話（二）

A: This is the dentist´s office. How may I help you?
B: Hello, my name is Ding Hui. I feel sick.
A: What´s the matter?
B: I have a toothache.
A: Do you want to make an appointment?
B: Yes, I do.
A: Can you come in this afternoon at 4 o´clock?
B: Sure. Thank you.
A: You´re welcome.
B: Good-bye.
A: Good-bye. See you at 4 o´clock.

生詞

dentist 牙醫

對話翻譯

A: 這裡是醫生診所，我能怎麼幫你嗎？
B: 你好，我叫丁慧，我不舒服。
A: 怎麼了？
B: 我牙疼。
A: 你想預約嗎？

B：想。
A：今天下午四點鐘來可以嗎？
B：可以， 謝謝。
A：不客氣。
B：再見。
A：再見。四點見。

對話（三）

A：Hello Ms. Ding.
B：Hello.
A：My name is Dr. Lee.
B：It is nice to meet you.
A：It is nice to meet you, too. I´m sorry that you are sick today.
B：Yes, I feel bad.
A：What´s the matter.
B：I have an earache.
A：Oh, really? I need to check your ears.
B：Okay.
A：You have an infection.
B：Oh!
A：Don´t worry. Here is some medicine.
B：Thank you.
A：Please take two pills every 4 hours.
B：Okay, I understand.
A：Good-bye.

B: Good-bye.

對話翻譯

A: 丁女士， 你好。
B: 你好。
A: 我是李醫生。
B: 很高興見到你。
A: 我也很高興見到你。
B: 真不幸你今天生病了。
A: 是呀，我不舒服。
B: 怎麼了？
A: 我耳朵疼。
B: 哦，是嗎？ 我得檢查一下你的耳朵。
A: 行。
B: 你的耳朵感染了。
A: 是嗎？
B: 別著急。 這是些藥。
A: 謝謝。
B: 請每隔四個小時吃兩粒。
A: 好，我懂了。
B: 再見。
A: 再見。

生詞

Ms. 女士

Dr. 醫生，博士， doctor 的縮寫
check 檢查
infection 感染
medicine 藥
pill 藥丸，藥粒

語法

英語的正式人稱稱呼

在正式場合下，講英語者常用姓來稱呼一個人，但在姓之前要加一個頭銜。在我們的對話裡，我們用了「Ms. Ding」 和 「Dr. Lee.」。「Ms.」是女士的意思，包括結婚的和不結婚的，「Miss」也是女士的意思，指沒結婚的或女孩。「Dr.」是醫生的正式稱呼，「Dr.」也有博士的意思。「Mr.」是成年男人的稱呼，包括結婚的和沒結婚的。「Mrs.」是夫人的意思，一聽就知道是結婚的。

複合句

複合句是由一個或一個以上的從句構成。主句為句子的主體，從句只用作句子的一個成分，從句不能獨立成為一個句子，雖然它有主語和謂語。從句常由關聯詞引導，並由關聯詞把從句和主句聯繫在一起。例如 I´m sorry that you are sick today. 就是一個複合句。I´m sorry 是主句， that 是關聯詞， you are sick today 是從句。

對話解釋

「Take two pills」吃兩粒藥。「every 4 hours」每四小時，有時你會聽到「once every 4 hours」意思是每四小時一次。你拿藥的時候，一定要聽清藥劑師告訴你怎麼吃。有些藥一定要在固定的時間吃。有的人對一些藥過敏，有的藥有副作用，可能引起其他的病。這些大家都要注意。

練習

I. 用正確的答案和問題搭配在一起

1) I have a headache. ______
2) Sure. You can come tomorrow at 11:30 in the morning. ______
3) You need to take 2 pills every 4 hours. ______
4) My right leg. ______
5) My date of birth is August 14th 1967. ______

A) May I make an appointment?
B) Where does it hurt?
C) What is your date of birth?
D) What do I need to do?
E) What´s the matter?

第二十八課 緊急情況（一） Emergencies (I)

對話（一）

A: Please help me.
B: What's the matter?
A: My friend is injured. He needs an ambulance.
B: Please tell me what happened.
A: We had a car accident. My friend can't move.
B: Don't worry. I'll call 9-1-1.
A: Thank you.
B: Where is your friend?
A: He's over there next to my car.
B: Okay, don't worry. Everything will be fine.

生詞

injured 受傷

ambulance 救護車
tell 告訴
me 我（賓格）
car 車
accident 事故，意外事件
car accident 車禍
had 有 have 過的去式
move 動
can´t 不能，can not 的縮寫
over there 在那邊

對話翻譯

A: 請幫我。
B: 怎麼了?
A: 我朋友受傷了，他需要救護車。
B: 請告訴我發生了什麼事。
A: 我們出車禍了。我朋友不能動了。
B: 別著急，我給 9-1-1 打電話。
A: 謝謝。
B: 你朋友在哪呢?
A: 他在我的車旁邊。
B: 好，別擔心，一切都會沒事的。

對話解釋

「had」是「have」的過去式。英語中表達過去發生的事

情要用過去式，過去式的構成我們以後再講。「We had a car accident.」意思是我們出車禍了。Everything will be fine. 一切都會沒事的。在發生緊急情況時，對發生的事情有一個積極的看法，安慰當事人很重要，害怕和著急只能把事情搞糟。

語法

代詞

me 在句子裡是賓語，賓語是接受動作的人或物。英語的人稱代詞有兩組，一組是主語代詞，我們已經學過了，「I, you , he, she, we, and they」還有一組是賓語代詞。比如說請給我「Please give me」me 是「我」的賓格，這和漢語不一樣，漢語的「我」不論在句子裡做什麼語都是「我」這個字。我們這個對話裡的句子「Please tell me」就是這樣，意思是請告訴我。「What happened」意思是發生了什麼。「Please tell me what happened.」 請告訴我發生了什麼。

一般過去式（一）

一般過去式表示過去發生的動作或狀態。 如果一件事從開始到結束都發生在過去，比如昨天，五分鐘以前，這句話裡的動詞就要用過去時態。用英語表達過去的動作時，除了用句子中表示時間的詞以外，句子中的動詞也要發生變化，要把動詞變成過去式。

規則動詞的一般過去式的構成：

動詞後面加 ed, 例如：
work - worked, happen - happened,

以 e 結尾的動詞後面只加 d， 例如：
move - moved, injure - injured

以 y 結尾的動詞如果 y 前邊是元音，動詞後面直接加 ed. 例如：
play - played, delay - delayed.
其他以 y 結尾的動詞要把 y 去掉，變成 i 然後加 ed.
例如：worry - worried, study - studied

還有一些不規則的動詞，這些動詞的變化不一，要逐個記。例如：
write - wrote, read - read, run - ran.

動詞	肯定	否定	疑問
be	I was a student. You were a student. He / She was a student. We / You / They were students.	I was not a student. You were not a student. He / She was not a student. We / You / They were not students.	Were you a student? Was he a student? Were you students? Were they students?
have	人稱代詞 + had pens	人稱代詞 + did not have pens	Did + 人稱代詞 + have pens?
study	人稱代詞 + studied English	人稱代詞 + did not study English	Did + 人稱代詞 + study English?

下面介紹一些有關醫療緊急情況的詞彙和句子：

choking 窒息，有異物卡在喉嚨裡

He´s choking. 他窒息了。

bleeding 出血

I´m bleeding. 我出血了。

broken 折斷的

I have a broken leg. 我的腿斷了。

burn 燒傷

She has a burn. 她燒傷了。

unconscious 昏迷

He´s unconscious. 他昏迷了。

對話（二）

A: Hello, 9-1-1 emergency.

B: My house is on fire!

A: What is your name please?

B: My name is Ding Hui.

A: What is your address Ms. Ding.

B: I live at 1426 Main Street in Chinatown.

A: Don´t worry. The fire department is on the way.

生詞

emergency 緊急情況

house 房子

fire 火
on fire 著火
on the way 在路上
address 地址
live 住
department 部門
fire department 救火站

對話翻譯

A: 你好，9－1－1緊急救護。
B: 我的房子著火了！
A: 你叫什麼名字？
B: 我叫丁慧。
A: 丁女士，你的地址是什麼？
B: 我住在中國城 1426 Main Street 。
A: 別著急，救護車馬上就上路。

對話解釋

你在給 9-1-1 打電話時，要先說你的名字，地址或地點、電話號碼，然後再說是什麼事。你說得越準確急救人員就來得越快。即使你的英語不太好，你也可以打 9-1-1。因為警察局的電腦裡能根據你的電話號碼查出你的住址。他們同樣會來。「my house is on fire」是我的房子著火了。這個表達很有趣，「on」是個介詞，意思是在什麼上，比如說「the pen is on the table」筆在桌上。on fire 是個詞組，著火。

練習

I. 把下面的句子譯成英文

1) 我朋友受傷了。
2) 她在流血。
3) 我的房子燒火了。
4) 我需要救護車。
5) 他的腿斷了。

第二十九課 緊急情況(二) Emergencies(II)

對話(一)

A: Excuse me, officer.
B: Yes, what's the matter?
A: I lost my son.
B: When?
A: 10 minutes ago.
B: What is your son's name?
A: His name is John.
B: How old is he?
A: He is 6 years old.
B: What is he wearing?
A: He is wearing a white t-shirt, blue shorts, and red tennis shoes.
B: What color is his hair?

A: His hair is black.
B: Where did you see him last?
A: I lost him in the toy store.
B: Okay, let´s go there.

生詞

officer 警官，警察先生 （對警察的禮貌稱呼）
lost 丟失， lose 的過去式
son 兒子
shorts 短褲
tennis 網球
tennis shoes 網球鞋
hair 頭髮
did 助動詞，是「do」的過去式
him he的賓格
last 最後
toy 玩具
store 商店
toy store 玩具店

對話翻譯

A: 對不起，警察先生。
B: 嗯，怎麼了？
A: 我把我兒子丟了。
B: 什麼時候丟的？

A: 十分鐘之前。
B: 你兒子叫什麼名字？
A: 他叫約翰。
B: 他幾歲了？
A: 他六歲。
B: 他穿什麼衣服？
A: 他穿白色T－恤衫，藍短褲和紅色網球鞋。
B: 他頭髮是什麼顏色？
A: 他頭髮是黑色。
B: 你最後是在哪看見他的？
A: 我是在玩具店把他丟了的。
B: 好，我們去那吧。

對話解釋

「officer」 警官，這是對警察的禮貌稱呼。西方國家的警察一般都經過了很好的訓練，非常職業化。在發生事故或緊急情況的時候，一般都是警察第一個到場，他們還會對出事者進行搶救。所以你見到警察的時候，你就可以說「Hello, officer」 或者 「excuse me, officer」。

「lost」是「lose」這個詞的過去式，多數的動詞過去式變化是有規律的。沒有規律的動詞只好一個一個地記了，「lost」這個詞就是其中的一個。例子：

I´m lost. 我走丟了。 也有「我糊塗了」的意思。

I lost my money. 我丟了錢。

對話（二）

A: Police! Call the police!
B: What´s the matter?
A: I´ve been robbed.
B: Oh, really? I´m sorry.
A: They took my money and my passport.
B: That´s terrible.

生詞

robbed 被搶劫
money 錢
passport 護照
took 是take的過去式，拿
Police 警察

對話翻譯

A: 警察！叫警察！
B: 怎麼了？
A: 我被搶劫了。
B: 哦，是嗎？很遺憾。
A: 他們把我的錢和護照搶走了。
B: 那太可怕了！

對話解釋

「robbed」是被搶劫的意思。「I´ve been robbed」我被搶劫了。這個句子的語法很複雜，以後再講。你們只記住這句話的意思就行了。

下面介紹一些在緊急情況下用的詞和句子。

I don´t understand. 我不懂。

I don´t speak English. 我不講英語。

I´m lost. 我走丟了。

Please help me. 請幫我。

I need an ambulance. 我需要一臺救護車。

I need a doctor. 我需要看醫生。

I need the police. 我需要找警察。

I need to contact the Chinese Embassy. 我需要和中國大使館聯繫。

練習

I. 用正確的答案和問題搭配在一起

1) I´ve been robbed. ________

2) My son is wearing blue pants and a yellow shirt. __________

3) She is 5 years old. _______

4) Sure I can. ________

5) I want to call the police. ________

A) What do you want to do?
B) What happened?
C) How old is she?
D) Can you help me?
E) What is he wearing?

第三十課 家庭 Family

對話(一)

A：Hello, Lee Ren De.

B：Hi, Ding Hui.

A：Do you have any brothers and sisters?

B：Yes, I do. I have 1 brother and 2 sisters.

A：Oh, really? What do they do?

B: My brother is a lawyer. My sisters are both teachers.

A：That´s interesting.

B：Thank you.

生詞

brother 兄弟，弟弟，哥哥
sister 姐妹，妹妹，姐姐
lawyer 律師
both 兩者
teacher 教師

對話翻譯

A: 你好，李仁德。
B: 你好，丁慧。
A: 你有兄弟姐妹嗎？
B: 有。我有一個哥哥，兩個妹妹。
A: 哦，是嗎？他們都幹什麼工作？
B: 我的哥哥是律師，我的兩個妹妹是教師。
A: 那很有意思。
B: 謝謝。

對話解釋

大家注意，英語中對家庭成員和親戚的稱呼不像漢語那麼細，而漢語一聽就能聽出來是哪邊的親戚，是父親家的，還是母親家的。如果你想知道是父親家的親戚還是母親家的親戚，你還得細問。

下面介紹一下有關家庭成員和親戚的名詞

father 父親，爸爸
mother 母親，媽媽
son 兒子
daughter 女兒
brother 兄弟，弟弟，哥哥
sister 姐妹，妹妹，姐姐
grandmother 祖母，外祖母，姥姥，奶奶
grandfather 祖父，外祖父，老爺，爺爺
aunt 姨媽，姑媽，舅媽
uncle 叔叔，伯伯，舅舅

對話（二）

A：Hello, Lee Ren De.
B：Hi, Ding Hui.
A：Where are you going?
B：I′m going to the hospital.
A：Why?
B：My grandfather is sick.
A：Oh, really? What′s the matter?
B：He has an ear infection.
A：That′s terrible.
B：Yes, it is.
A：Give him my best.
B：I will. Thank you.

對話翻譯

A: 你去哪兒?
B: 我去醫院。
A: 幹什麼去?
B: 我的爺爺(老爺)病了。
A: 是嗎? 怎麼了?
B: 他耳朵發炎了。
A: 那可真不好。
B: 是呀。
A: 代我向他問好
B: 我會的，謝謝。

對話解釋

Give him my best. 代我向他問好。best 是最好的意思。這是美國人常說的一句問候別人的話，如果這個人不在場，你想讓別人代問他／她好，就用這個句子。

對話（三）

A: I need to go to the store.
B: Why?
A: My mother wants some ice cream.
B: When do you want to go?
A: Now. Would you like to come with me?
B: Sure. My uncle wants some apples.

A: Do you have money?
B: Yes I do.
A: Okay, let´s go.
B: You can drive.
A: No problem.

生詞

now 現在
with 和誰一起，和誰一塊兒
with me 和我一起

對話翻譯

A: 我得去商店。
B: 幹什麼去？
A: 我媽媽想要冰淇淋。
B: 你想什麼時候去？
A: 現在就去。你想跟我一起去嗎？
B: 好哇。我叔叔想要些蘋果。
A: 你有錢嗎？
B: 我有。
A: 好，我們走吧。
B: 你開車吧。
A: 沒問題。

對話解釋

Would you like to come with me? 你願意跟我一起來嗎? 這是很有禮貌的邀請別人一起做什麼的一種說法。You can drive. 你開車吧。這是有禮貌的命令。如果說「You drive」這個命令的口氣就太生硬了。如果你把動詞的聲音說得很大，如「Go」「Stop」就是很嚴肅的命令。

練習

I. 閱讀下面的短文並回答問題

John has a nice family. His father´s name is Andy. Andy is 74 years old. Andy likes to play chess in the park. John also has 1 sister. She is a doctor in the city hospital. John doesn´t have any children. His sister has a son and a daughter. The son is 9 years old. The daughter is 11 years old. They both like to watch TV and eat ice cream.

1) What does John´s sister do?
2) Who is Andy?
3) What does Andy like to do?
4) Does John have any children?
5) How old is John´s sister´s son?

你上週末做什麼了?(一)
What Did You Do Last Weekend?(I)

對話

A: Hi, Lee Ren De. How was your weekend?

B: It was great!

A: What did you do?

B: I went to the park with my family on Saturday.

A: Oh, really?

B: Yes, it was a beautiful sunny day.

A: What else did you do?

B: We played volleyball. We also ate hamburgers.

A: That´s interesting.

B: What did you do last weekend?

A: I watched TV.
B: What else did you do?
A: I washed my clothes.
B: That´s boring.

生詞

weekend 週末
went 去，go 的過去時
beautiful 美麗的，漂亮的
volleyball 排球
ate 吃，eat 的過去式
hamburger 漢堡包
did 助動詞 do 的過去式，只起語法作用
boring 令人厭煩的，沒意思的
else 其他的
cloth 衣服

對話翻譯

A: 嗨，李仁德，你週末過得好嗎？
B: 好極了。
A: 你都幹什麼了？
B: 週六我和我家裡人去公園了。
A: 哦，是嗎？
B: 是呀， 那天是艷陽天。
A: 你還幹什麼了？

B: 我們打排球。我們還吃漢堡了。
A: 很有意思。
B: 你上週末幹什麼了?
A: 我看電視了。
B: 你還幹什麼了?
A: 我洗衣服了。
B: 那真沒意思。

語法:

一般過去時態(二)

be 的人稱和數的變化

和一般現在時態一樣,be 要隨著人稱和數來變化。第一人稱單數和第三人稱單數用 was, 其餘用 were.
例如:
I was a student. It was great! Tom was a lawyer. You were wonderful. We were all students. They were students, too.

一般過去時態的否定式和疑問式

除動詞 be 外,各種動詞的否定句和疑問句中的動詞變化和一般現在時態一樣。
例如:I went to school yesterday. He did not go to school yesterday. Did you go to school yesterday?

過去時態並不那麼難，知道事情發生的時間能幫助選用正確的時態。從語法上說，表示時間的詞可以放在句子的前面也可以放在後面。但不能放在句子的中間。如果我們想強調時間的話，就把時間放在前面，否則，一般都放在句子的後邊。

例如：

Yesterday I went to the store.

I went to the store yesterday.

這兩句話都對，你可以把「yesterday」放在句子的前邊，也可以放在句子的後邊。我們再看幾個例子：

On Sunday I washed my clothes.

I washed my clothes on Sunday.

這兩句話也都對。這句話的時間是「On Sunday」，「on」這個字用在某一天的前面。

動詞	肯定	否定	疑問
be	I was a student. You were a student He / She was a student. We / You / They were students	I was not a student. You were not a student. He / She was not a student. We / You / They were not students.	Were you a student? Was he a student? Were you students? Were they students?
have	人稱代詞 + had pens	人稱代詞 + did not have pens	Did + 人稱代詞 + have pens?
study	人稱代詞 + studied English.	人稱代詞 + did not study English	Did + 人稱代詞 + study English?

對話解釋

「was」是「be」的過去式。「did」是「do」的過去式。「What do you do?」這個問題是問別人做什麼工作。「What did you do?」是問別人過去做了什麼。「went」是「go」的過去式。「ate」是「eat」的過去式。

如果你想說禮拜一你做什麼了，你可以說「On Monday, I did something」。

當我們說具體時間的時候，前邊要用「at」。
At 6 o´clock I watched TV.
I watched TV at 6 o´clock.

在月份前要用 「in」
In August I went to Taipei.
I went to Taipei in August.

練習

I. 用動詞的過去式填空

1) Yesterday Mary and Tom __________ basketball. (play)
2) John _______ to school last week. (go)
3) We _________ TV for 6 hours. (watch)
4) My mother _______ sick. (be)
5) Jennifer _______ a hamburger for dinner yesterday. (eat)

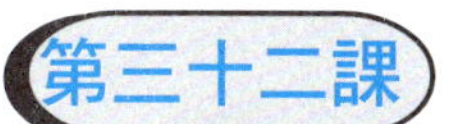

第三十二課 你上週末做什麼了？(二)
What Did You Do Last Weekend?(II)

對話（一）

A: Where were you on Sunday?
B: I went to New York.
A: Oh, really? Why?
B: I visited my grandmother. It was her birthday.
A: That was nice. How old is she?
B: She is 90 years old.
A: Wow!

生詞

visit 參觀，訪問，看
birthday 生日

Wow 哇

對話翻譯

A: 你星期日在哪？
B: 我去紐約了。
A: 哦是嗎？ 去幹什麼了？
B: 我去看了我的奶奶（姥姥）了。那天是她的生日。
A: 那很好啊。他多大年齡了？
B: 她九十歲了。
A: 哇！

對話解釋

Where were you on Sunday? 你星期日在哪?「were」是「be」的過去式。「were」這個字放在「you」你、你們、或許多人，「They」 或 「we」的後面。其他代詞 I, she, he, it 或單數名詞後方接「was」。
比如:

Where were you on Sunday? 你星期日在哪?
Where was she on Sunday? 她星期日在哪?
Where were they on Sunday? 他們星期日在哪?
I visited my grandmother. 我去看了我的奶奶。
It was her birthday. 那天是她的生日。
「Birthday」生日。這是個很常用的字。生日這首歌很流行，並被翻譯成多種文字 。

歌詞

The Birthday Song

Happy Birthday to you.
Happy Birthday to you.
Happy Birthday dear students. (students 可以改成任何人)
Happy Birthday to you.

下面的兩句話雖然是一起說的，但時態不一樣。That was nice. 是指B去紐約這件事情，這是以前發生的事，所以用過去式。「How old is she?」是現在式，我們問別人現在的年齡的時候，用現在式。Wow! 這個字表示激動或令人驚異。人能活到 90 歲確實是件不尋常的事情。

對話（二）

A: John, did you clean your room?
B: Yes, I did.
A: How about your homework?
B: I finished half of it.
A: Let me have a look.
B: OK, here you are.

生詞

clean 打掃
room 房間
how about ...怎麼樣? 你以為…怎麼樣？
homework 作業
finish 完成
look 看
have a look 看一看

對話翻譯

A: 約翰，你打掃你的房間了嗎?
B: 我打掃了。
A: 你的作業怎麼樣了?
B: 我做完了一半。
A: 讓我看看。
B: 好啊，給你。

對話解釋

John, did you clean your room? 「did」是「do」的過去式，在這裡是助動詞，只起語法作用。句子中的動詞用原形，也就是字典裡的形式。因為did這個字已經說明了句子的時態，所以句子中的動詞用原形就行了。這句話的意思是約翰，你打掃你的房間了嗎?
我們可以用這個句型問很多問題。例如：

Did he wash his clothes? 他洗衣服了嗎?
Did they play basketball? 他們打球了嗎?
Did you go to the store? 你去商店了嗎?
Did she eat the apple? 她吃蘋果了嗎?
Did my brother write the letter? 我弟弟寫信了嗎?

回答這些問題很容易。

Yes, I did.
No, I didn´t.

How about your homework? How about 是個詞組，意思是...怎麼樣? (你以為)…如何? How about your homework? 就是你的作業怎麼樣了? 或你做作業了嗎?
have a look是個詞組，看一看，Let me have a look. 讓我看一看。這句話非常有用。OK, here you are. 好，給你。把東西給別人時，一般都說Here you are.

對話（三）

A: Hello, Lee Ren De.
B: Hi, Ding Hui.
A: What are you doing?
B: I´m playing cards.

A: I played cards yesterday.
B: Oh, really? With who?
A: I played cards with my Mother and Father.
B: That´s great. I play cards everyday. I like cards.

生詞

card 撲克牌

對話翻譯

A: 喂，李仁德。
B: 嗨，丁慧。
A: 你幹什麼呢？
B: 我打撲克呢。
A: 我昨天打撲克了。
B: 哦，是嗎？和誰打的？
A: 和我父母打的。
B: 那太好了。我每天都打撲克。 我喜歡打撲克。

對話解釋

I´m playing cards. 這是現在進行式。我們用這個時態表示現在正在發生的事情。I played cards yesterday. 這句話是過去式，我們一看「yesterday」就知道是過去發生的事情了。I play cards everyday.

這是一般現在式。一般現在式表示常發生的事。everyday 這個字也能告訴你這是經常發生的事。

這個對話裡有一個新的問題，就是 With who? 「who」誰，「with」和...誰在一起。「With who?」 的意思就是和誰玩。

練習

I. 用正確的答案和問題搭配在一起

1) It was under the chair. ______
2) Yes, I did. All my clothes are clean now. ______
3) Yesterday I visited my grandmother. ________
4) On Sunday she went to the park. _______
5) No, I didn´t. I´m hungry. ______

A) Did you eat breakfast?
B) What did you do yesterday?
C) Where was your book?
D) What did Mary do on Sunday?
E) Did you wash your clothes?

第三十三課 在郵局裡(一) At the Post Office (I)

對話 (一)

A: Yes, sir, can I help you?

B: Hi, how are you?

A: Pretty good. How about yourself?

B: Excellent. I´d like to send this letter to China

A: To China, OK. How soon would you like it to be there, sir?

B: What are my options?

生詞

sir 先生

pretty 很，相當，好看

pretty good 很好
yourself 你自己
excellent 好極了
send 寄，送
how soon 多快
option 選擇
global 國際的，全球的
express 特快傳遞
priority 優先的
normal 正常的，平常的
airmail 航空郵件

對話翻譯

A: 先生你好，我能幫你嗎?
B: 嗨，你好嗎？
A: 很好，你自己呢？
B: 好極了。我想把這封信寄到中國。
A: 到中國，好。你想多快寄到那裡，先生？
B: 我的選擇是什麼？

對話解釋

「Sir」是先生的意思。這個字是對男人尊敬的稱呼，如果我們不知道男人的姓，一般都用這個字來稱呼。如果知道，可以用「Mr.」 後面加姓就可以了。如果是女的，我們叫 「 Ma´am」。「How about yourself?」

是問別人怎麼樣的一種禮貌說法。「to China」 裡的to表示地點，放在表示地點詞的前邊。「how soon」多快，「it」是個代詞，在這裡指信，「to be there」意思是到那裡。How soon would you like it to be there, sir? 你想多快寄到那裡，先生？

對話（二）

A: Yes, may I help you?
B: Yes, I´d like to send this letter to China.
A: Okay, how soon would you like it to be there?
B: Please send it by normal airmail.
A: No problem. That costs 80 cents.
B: Here you are.
A: Thank you. Have a nice day.
B: You, too. Good-bye.

生詞

by 用...手段，方法

對話翻譯

A: 先生你好，我能幫你嗎?
B: 是的，我想把這封信寄到中國。

A: 好。你想多快寄到那裡？
B: 請用一般航空郵件寄。
A: 沒問題。 一共80美分。
B: 錢在這裡。
A: 謝謝。祝你有個愉快的一天。
B: 你也是。再見。

對話解釋

Please send it by normal airmail. 請用一般的航空郵件寄。「by」在句子裡的意思是用... 手段。

練習

I. 把下面的句子譯成漢語
1) I´m going to the post office.
2) That costs 50 cents.
3) What are my options?
4) I want to send this letter to my grandmother.
5) Please send it by normal airmail.

第三十四課 在郵局裡(二) At the Post Office (II)

對話

A: Yes, sir, can I help you?

B: Hi, how are you?

A: Pretty good, how about yourself?

B: Excellent. I´d like to send this letter to China

A: To China, OK. How soon would you like it to be there, sir?

B: What are my options?

A: OK, take a look at the screen right here. Just a moment. Here we go. If you send it by global express, it is $19.00. If you send it by global priority, that will be

$5.00. If you send it by normal airmail, it costs eighty cents.

B: Well, let´s go cheap. I don´t have a lot of money.

A: That´s 80 cents. We can do it. Would you like a stamp on it or a meter strip?

B: Stamp.

A: OK, I will get two 40-cent stamps for you.

B: Thank you.

A: Here are a couple of 40-cent stamps. Just go ahead and put them on if you would like.

生詞

screen 屏幕，電視屏幕，電腦屏幕
look 看
take a look 看一下，看一看
right 正好的，恰好的
right here 就這兒（地點更確切）
just a moment 等一下
here we go 我們開始吧
if 如果
send 郵寄
by 靠什麼方法，手段
global priority 國際優先郵件（是僅次於global express 國際特快傳遞）
cheap 便宜

meter 測量儀器，測量表，馬路上的停車表

strip 條帶，長條

meter strip 用機器打出來的標籤

stamp 郵票

a couple of 兩個

just go ahead 就這樣做吧，就幹吧

put 放在什麼上或貼

them 他們（在對話裡指郵票）

put on 把什麼放在…上，穿上

對話翻譯

A: 先生你好，我能幫你嗎?

B: 嗨，你好嗎？

A: 很好啊，你自己呢？

B: 好極了。我想把這封信寄到中國。

A: 到中國，好。你想多快寄到那裡，先生？

B: 我的選擇是什麼？

A: 好，看看這的螢光屏。等一下。我們開始吧。如果你寄國際特快，是 19 美元。如果你寄國際優先件，是 5 美元。如果你寄平件，是 80 美分。

B: 嗯，還是來便宜的吧。我的錢不多。

A: 那是 80 美分。我們可以這樣做。你想在信封上貼郵票還是打標籤？

B: 貼郵票。

A: 好，我給你四十美分的郵票。

B: 謝謝。

A: 好。這是兩張 40 美分的郵票。如果你想的話，就把它貼上吧。

對話解釋

在美國郵局寄信或寄包裹有很多不同的方法。你可以多交些錢，你寄的東西就會在一兩天之內到達。無論是國內還是國際的。你也可以寄掛號信，保證對方能收到。往中國寄信，有三個選擇，這幾個選擇的不同就是信寄到中國的時間不同。越早寄到，花錢就越多。「What are my options?」我的選擇是什麼? Global express 這是第一個選擇，國際特快傳遞。如果你有封信，必須在一兩天內寄到中國的話，你就得用「global express」。「global priority」是第二個選擇。「priority」的意思是優先的，需要優先考慮的事物。這是在郵局寄信第二快的郵件。「Global priority」可翻成國際優先。這個服務比 Global express 便宜很多。往中國寄信可能一個星期左右能到。 Normal airmail 這是第三個也是最便宜的選擇，也就是航空郵件。但並不一定快，也許要兩個星期才能到。

語法

條件句

If you send it by normal airmail, it costs 80 cents. 如果你寄平件，是 80 美分。

我們把這樣的句子叫做條件句。 條件句一般有兩部份，一部份是假設的條件，一部份是根據條件得出的結果。假設條件的部分一般由 if 開始。

練習

I. 把兩句話用「if」合併成一個條件句

1) You send it by Global Priority. That will be $5.00.
If you send it by Global Priority, that will be $5.00.
2) He is happy. He will smile.
3) They are hungry. They can eat apples.
4) You are tired. You can go to sleep.
5) She had money. She would buy a new dress.

II. 用括號裡適當的詞填空 (if, or, by, let´s).

1) Do you want to see a movie _____ watch TV?
2) He goes to work _____ taxi everyday.
3) ______ go to the park.
4) Would you like an apple ______ some ice cream?
5) _____ eat. I´m hungry.

第三十五課 在郵局裡（三） At the Post office(III)

對話

B: I´d like to buy a book of stamps.

A: A book of stamps? We can do that. Any particular design?

B: No, that´s OK. US flags.

A: We got that. Any phone cards or anything today?

B: No, thank you.

A: That´s 20 of the United States Flag stamps. That will be $7.60 all together.

B: $7.60. Out of $20.00.

A: Out of 20 that will be fine. You can also use your credit or debit cards, we´ll take checks with ID, but cash is always good, too.

B: Cash is the best.

A: $13.40 is your change. That´s $7.60, 70, 75, 80, 9, 10 and 10 makes $20. Here is the receipt for you. Thank you, sir.

B: Have a good day.

A: Thank you very much. Yes, sir, may I help you.

生詞與詞組

A book of 一本
particular 特殊的
design 圖案，設計
flag 旗
phone cards 電話卡
anything 什麼事，什麼物
all 全部，所有
all together 全部，一共
out 向外，在外
out of 從.....裡頭，從....當中
credit 信用，貸款
credit card 信用卡
debit 借方
debit card 借用卡
check 支票

ID 身份證，是「identification」的縮寫
receipt 收據

對話翻譯

B: 我想買一本郵票。
A: 一本郵票？可以。要特殊的圖案嗎？
B: 不用，美國國旗的就行了。
A: 那我們有。還要不要電話卡和什麼別的東西？
B: 不要，謝謝。
A: 那就是20張美國國旗的郵票。一共七塊六。
B: 七塊六。我從這二十塊錢拿出七塊六(二十塊錢給你找)。
A: 二十塊，好。你也可以用信用卡或借用卡付錢。如果你有身份證，我們也收支票，但是現金也很好。
B: 現金最好了。
A: 13塊4是找你的錢。好，七塊六，七…九塊，十塊和十塊，一共二十塊。這是你的收據，先生，謝謝你。
B: 祝你有個愉快的一天。
A: 非常感謝。先生，我可以幫你嗎？

對話解釋

B在買一本郵票。一本郵票有20張郵票，英語叫「 a book of stamps」。 Any phone cards or anything today? 這是一句省略句。全句應該是「Do you want any phone cards or anything else today?」人們在講話的時侯多用省略句。意思是說「還要不要電話卡或什麼別的東西？」我們可能都用電話卡給家人打電話，特別是打國際電話，用電話卡打很便宜。郵局也賣電話卡。$7.60. Out of $20.00. out of 是個詞組是從…裡頭，從…當中的意思。這句話是說「我從這二十塊錢拿出七塊六」。credit card 是信用卡的意思。debit card 是借用卡。用 debit card 的時候，就像開出一張支票，錢直接從你的銀行提出去了。美國人喜歡使用credit cards 和 debit cards，這樣他們就不用身上帶著很多錢。帶錢太多危險。I D 是「identification」的縮寫，身份證，身份證上一般有照片，可以是駕駛執照，或護照。

練習

I. 把兩句話用「or」合併成一個句子

1) Would you like any phone cards today? Would you like anything today?
   Would you like any phone cards or anything today?
2) Would you like an apple? Would you like an orange?
3) Do you want to dance? Do you want to watch TV?
4) Is she happy? Is she sad?
5) Can we play basketball? Can we play soccer?

房屋 Housing

對話（一）

A：Hello, Ding Hui.

B：Hi, Lee.

A：Where are you going?

B：I´m going home.

A：Where do you live?

B：I have a house in the suburbs.

A：That sounds nice.

B：Yes it is. I have a big yard with trees and a garden.

生詞

home 家，住的家
house 房子，一般指獨立的房子。
suburb 郊區，離城市比較近的地方
sound 原本是「聲音」的意思，這裡是指「聽起來」
big 大
yard 院子
trees 樹
garden 花園

對話翻譯

A: 丁慧，你好。
B: 李，你好。
A: 你去哪？
B: 我回家。
A: 你住哪？
B: 我在郊區有棟房子。
A: 聽起來很好。
B: 對，是很好。我有一個大院子，院裡有樹和花園。

對話解釋

「house」一般指獨立的房子。 「suburb」 郊區，離城市比較近的地方。美國人多數都有車，所以那些在城裡工作的人不一定住在城裡。如果他們有錢，很多人都自己買棟房子，開車上班。一天都要開一個多小時的車上下班。

對話（二）

A: Hello, Lee Ren De.
B: Hi, Ding Hui.
A: Where are you going?
B: I´m going home.
A: Where do you live?
B: I have a one bedroom apartment in the city.
A: That sounds nice.
B: Yes it is. My apartment is big. It also has a kitchen, living room, bathroom, walk-in closet, and a balcony.

生詞

bedroom 臥室
apartment 公寓
city 城市
kitchen 廚房
living room 客廳
bathroom 洗手間
balcony 陽臺
walk-in 人能走得進去
closet 壁櫥

walk-in closet 人能走進去的壁櫥

對話翻譯

A: 李仁德，你好。
B: 丁慧，你好。
A: 你去哪？
B: 我回家。
A: 你住哪？
B: 我在市裡有個一室一廳的公寓。
A: 聽起來很好。
B: 對，是很好。我的公寓很大，裡面還有廚房、客廳、臥室、人能走進去的壁櫥和涼台。

對話解釋

one bedroom apartment 這是說B的公寓有一個臥室。美國人根據房子的大小，有多少臥室來確定房子或公寓的價錢。你看到有關房子的廣告時，一般都先寫有幾間臥室。比如有兩個臥室的房子，三個臥室的房子。

City 是城市的意思。如果誰說他住在城裡，他的意思通常是他住在離高樓大廈很近的市中心。市中心沒有很多地能蓋住房，特別是有院子，有樹的房子。所以住在市裡的人一般都住在公寓樓裡。

介紹一些有關房間裡的傢具和用具的詞

kitchen 廚房
bedroom 臥室
living room 客廳
bathroom 洗澡間
stove 爐子
bed 床
sofa 沙發
toilet 廁所
sink 水池
dresser 梳妝臺
TV 電視
cabinets 櫃
mirror 鏡子
telephone 電話
medicine cabinet 醫藥櫃
table 桌子
closet 壁櫥
coffee table 咖啡桌
refrigerator 冰箱
shower 淋浴
dishwasher 洗碗機
bathtub 浴池

練習

1. 用「,」和「and」把幾個句子連在一起，寫成一個句子。
   1) He has a dog. He has a horse. He has a cow. He has a pig.
      He has a dog, horse, cow, and a pig.
   2) Mary wants a house. Mary wants a car. Mary wants a bicycle.
   3) Let´s go to the park. Let´s go to the post office. Let´s go to the bank. Let´s go to the store.
   4) Her apartment has a kitchen. Her apartment has a bedroom. Her apartment has a balcony.
   5) I want to eat a hamburger. I want to eat a salad. I want to eat some oranges.

第三十七課 租公寓(一) Renting an Apartment(I)

對話(一)

A：Hello, this is Comfort Apartments. How may I help you?

B：Yes, I´m looking for a place to live.

A：We have one and two bedroom apartments available.

B：How much is a two bedroom apartment?

A：It is 950 dollars a month plus utilities.

B：How much is a one bedroom apartment?

A：It is 650 a month plus utilities.

生詞

rent 用作動詞是「租」，用作名詞是「房租」

comfort 舒服

comfortable 舒服的

look for 找

place 地方

live 住

available 可使用的，可利用的。

plus 外加，付加的，這個字也用在數學上，是加的意思。

utilities 公用事業，公用設施，或公用事業提供服務，一般是指水電煤氣等費用。

對話翻譯

A: 你好，這裡是舒服公寓，我能幫你嗎？

B: 是的，我在找住的地方。

A: 我們有一室一廳和兩室一廳的公寓。

B: 兩室一廳的公寓房租多少錢？

A: 兩個臥室的房租是 950 美元，加上水電費。

B: 一室一廳公寓房租多少錢？

A: 一個臥室的房租是 650 美元，加上水電費。

對話解釋

comfortable 是 comfort 的形容詞，舒服的， -able 是個結尾的後綴，英語有很多形容詞用這個結尾。如：disable, enjoyable, irritable 等。「I´m looking for」的意思是我正在找什麼。look for 是個很

常用的詞組。比如說 I´m looking for my father。我在找我的爸爸，I´m looking for my pen. 我在找我的筆。utilities 是公用事業，公用設施，或公用事業提供服務，如水電煤氣等。有的公寓的房租包括這些服務，有的不包括，所以租房子的時候一定要問清。在你租房子的時候，公寓的管理人員會給你一個公用事業服務公司的名單，你自己決定用哪一家公司。

對話（二）

B：What utilities are included with the apartment?

A：Water is free, but you have to pay for electricity and your telephone.

B：So you have an electric stove and heat?

A：Yes, that´s right.

B：What electric company do you use.

A：We use the River Electric Company.

生詞

include 包括

free 免費

electricity 電

pay 交錢

have to 必須，不得不

but 但是

happy 高興
sad 不高興，傷心，沮喪
so 所以
electric 電
heat 熱氣，取煖
company 公司
use 用
river 河

對話翻譯

B: 公寓都包什麼公用設施費？
A: 水免費，但你得交電費和電話費。
B: 那麼你們有電爐和熱氣嗎？
A: 對。
B: 你們用什麼電器公司？
A: 我們用河電公司。

對話解釋

have to 是必須，不得不的意思。是個很常用的詞組。例如：
You have to wash your clothes. 你必須得洗衣服。
You have to cook dinner. 你必須得做飯。
I have to pay for electricity and your telephone. 我必須得交電錢，和電話費。
but 但是，這是個連接詞，把兩個句子聯起來，表示轉折。so所以，用在因果關係的句子裡。so後面句子的內容是根據前面的內容推理出來的。

練習

I. 把兩句話用「but」合併成一個句子

1) Water is free. You have to pay for electricity.

   Water is free, but you have to pay for electricity.

2) He has an English book. He can′t find it.

3) I′m hungry. I don′t have any food.

4) I need to buy a stamp. The post office is closed.

5) She wants to go to the movies. She is very busy.

第三十八課 租公寓(二) Renting an Apartment(II)

對話 (一)

A: Do you like the apartment?

B: Yes I do, but I have a few more questions.

A: What are they?

B: If something is broken, who do I call to fix it?

A: You can call our maintenance man.

B: Who will pay for it?

A: If you break the item, you will pay for it. If the item breaks by itself, we will pay for it.

B: Great. How long is the lease?

A: Our standard lease is for 12 months.

B: When can I move in?

A: You can move in tomorrow if you want.

生詞

a few 一些， 幾個
question 問題
something 東西，事情
broken 壞了，破碎了
fix 修理
maintenance 保養
maintenance man 修理工
break 損壞，打破
item 個別物體，東西，條款
how long 多長時間 多久
lease 租約
standard 標準的
standard lease 標準租約
move 搬家

對話翻譯

A: 你喜歡這個公寓嗎?
B : 喜歡，但我還有幾個問題。
A : 什麼問題?
B : 如果有東西壞了，我給誰打電話修理?
A : 你可以給我們的修理工打電話。
B : 誰花錢?

A：如果是你搞壞的，你花錢，如果是自己壞的，我們花。
B：太好了，租約是多長時間?
A：我們正常的租約是 12 個月。
B：我什麼時候可以搬進來?
A：如果你想的話，你明天就可以搬。

對話解釋

I have a few more questions. more 更多，在這裡是說 B 以前問過問題，但還有問題要問，所以就用了 more 這個字。意思是「我還有幾個問題」。如果說 I have a few questions. 這句話和前邊那句話就不同，意思是B以前沒有問過問題。standard lease 的意思是標準租約，也就是說房主給每個房客的租約都是固定不變的。大多數的租約都是一年，也就是十二個月。你如果想要在租約到期以前離開就很難。如果你必須得離開，你就得交付一年的房租。 簽租約也有個好處，就是簽了租約以後，房東就不能隨便讓你搬走，也不能隨便漲房租。

對話（二）

A：I want the one bedroom apartment.
B：Great! That will be 650 dollars a month.
A：No problem.
B：We also need a security deposit of 650

dollars.

A：So that comes to 1300 dollars right now.

B：That is correct.

A：I have a car. Is there a parking fee?

B：No, there isn´t. Each apartment has one free parking space.

A：That´s good.

B：Here is our standard lease for 12 months.

A：Okay.

B：Please read it and sign it at the bottom.

A：I´m finished. Here is your money.

B：Here is your key. You can move in at any time.

A：Thank you.

B：Have a nice day.

生詞

great 很好
security 安全
deposit 押金
security deposit 安全押金
that comes to 一共是
right now 現在
correct 正確的
parking 停車
parking fee 停車費

sign 簽字
bottom 底下
at the bottom 在底下
finished 完成了
key 鑰匙
any 任何
any time 何時間

對話翻譯

A: 我想要一個臥室的公寓。
B: 好， 一個月 650 美元。
A: 沒問題。
B: 我們還要收 650 美元的安全押金。
A: 所以現在一共是 1300 美元。
B: 沒錯。
A: 我有一台車，需要交停車費嗎？
B: 不用。每個公寓有一個免費的停車位。
A: 好。
B: 這是我們 12 個月標準的合同。
A: 好。
B: 請看一下，在這下面簽字。
A: 簽完了。這是給你的錢。
B: 這是鑰匙。你可以隨時搬進去。
A: 謝謝。
B: 祝你有個愉快的一天。

對話解釋

。

「security deposit」安全押金，這個押金在你的租約用完了以後房東才退給你。如果你在租約沒到期之前搬出去，或者把公寓裡的什麼東西搞壞了，房主就用這個錢來補。一般安全押金的數目和一個月的房租一樣多。所以在你搬進公寓時，你得準備兩個月的租金才行。有的房主還要求你在填申請表的同時，要你從你工作的公司開一份工作證明，證明你掙多少錢，能確保每月支付得起房租。 that comes to 是個詞組，意思是錢的總數是…。finished 是完成了的意思。這個字是動詞也是形容詞。許多美國人在他們做完一件事的時候常用這個字， I´m finished. 意思是我做完了。

練習

I. 閱讀下面的廣告，用完整的句子回答問題。

Now Leasing!
Luxury Apartments
2 Bedrooms (also includes a kitchen, bathroom, walk-in closet, and balcony)
$1500 a month plus utilities
One year lease
Free Parking

1) How long is the lease?
2) Is there a parking fee?
3) How many bedrooms are in the apartment?
4) Does the apartment have a balcony?
5) How much is the rent?

第三十九課 美國的節假日(一) Holidays(I)

對話（一）

A: Hello, Ding Hui.
B: Hi, Lee.
A: Halloween is next week.
B: Oh, really? What will you do?
A: I will go to a costume party.
B: What costume will you wear?
A: I will wear a cowboy costume.
B: What will you do at the party?
A: I will bob for apples and dance.
B: Sounds like fun.
A: Do you want to go?
B: Sure.

生詞

next week 下週
Halloween 萬聖節，鬼節
costume 服裝，這個服裝不是我們平時穿的服裝，而是舞台服裝，跳舞服裝化裝舞會的服裝等等。
party 聚會
cowboy 牛仔。這是個複合詞。cow 是牛的意思，boy 是男孩的意思。
bob 在水裡上下動
bob for apples 是美國人在萬聖節玩的一種遊戲
like 相像，像…一樣

對話翻譯

A: 丁慧，你好。
B: 李，你好 。
A: 下個星期是萬聖節。
B: 是嗎? 你想幹什麼?
A: 我去一個化裝聚會。
B: 你穿什麼化妝服？
A: 我穿牛仔服。
B: 你在聚會上都幹什麼?
A: 我要玩個蘋果的遊戲，還跳舞。
B: 聽起來好像挺有意思。
A: 你想去嗎?
B: 好啊。

語法

一般將來時態

一般將來時態表示將來發生的事情。將來式的構成是 will 加動詞的原型。

主語＋will ＋動詞原型

What will you do next week? 這句話用的是一般將來時態。因為是問將來要做的事。句子裡的 next week 是表示將來的時間。

動詞	肯定	否定	疑問
Be	I will be a student.	I will not be a student.	Will you be a student?
Have	I will have a pen.	I will not have a pen.	Will you have a pen?
Study	I will study English.	I will not study English.	Will you study English?

例子：

He will go to school next week.

下星期他去學校。

I will go to see my friend tomorrow.

明天我去看我的朋友。

I will wash my clothes on Sunday.
星期天我會洗衣服。
I will watch TV tonight.
我今晚看電視。

對話解釋

Sounds like fun. 聽起來好像挺有意思。這是個省略句。全句應是 It sounds like fun. like 這個字在這裡是好像的意思。例子:

He looks like my friend Pat. 他看上去像我的朋友帕特。
I feel like a bird. 我感覺像隻鳥。

Halloween萬聖節是在每年的十月三十日。這天美國人都要買些糖果，把這些糖放在一個大碗裡，然後把這個碗放在門旁邊，那天晚上小孩們一定會穿著各式各樣的衣服來敲你的門要糖吃。 你給孩子開門時，孩子們會說 Trick or Treat。Trick 的意思是戲法，把戲，詭計。Treat 的意思是款待，好吃的東西，比如糖果等等。這句話的意思是如果你不給我們糖吃我們就捉弄你。

語法

特殊疑問句

就句子中某一部分提問的疑問句，叫做特殊疑問句。特殊疑問句是以疑問詞開始的句子，回答時要具體，不能用 yes 和 no 來回答。這也是和一般疑問句的區別。疑問詞有what, who, where, when and how. 例如What will you do at the party? 你在聚會上都將幹什麼? 這句話是將來式的特殊疑問句。

特殊疑問句的構成有兩種。

第一種與陳述句的詞序相同。例如：

Who is there? 誰在那兒？
What is in the box? 盒子裡有什麼？
Which apple is my apple? 那個蘋果是我的蘋果？
How are you? 你好嗎？

第二種結構是 疑問詞 ＋ 一般疑問句的詞序

What are you doing? 你幹什麼呢？
Which do you want? 你要哪一個？

對話（二）

A: Hello, Ding Hui
B: Hi, Lee.
A: Thanksgiving is next Thursday.
B: Oh, really? What will you do?

A: I'll go to my grandmother's house.
B: What will you do at your grandmother's house?
A: My family will eat a big dinner.
B: What will you eat?
A: We'll eat turkey, stuffing, mashed potatoes, cranberry sauce, and have pumpkin pie for dessert.
B: Wow! Sounds like fun.
A: Do you want to come?
B: Sure.

生詞

Thanksgiving 感恩節
Thursday 星期四
big 大
dinner 正餐，晚餐
big dinner 大餐，其中有許多菜

感恩節時吃的食品

turkey 火雞
stuffing 添在食物中的餡
mash 搗碎，壓碎
potato 土豆（馬鈴薯）
mashed potatoes 土豆泥（馬鈴薯泥）
cranberry 在美國生長的一種草莓

sauce 食物調味品，果醬
cranberry sauce 在美國生長的一種草莓做成的果醬
pumpkin 南瓜
pie 餡餅
pumpkin pie 南瓜餡餅

對話翻譯

A: 丁慧，你好。
B: 你好，李。
A: 下星期四是感恩節。
B: 噢，是嗎?
A: 我要去我奶奶家。
B: 你去你奶奶家幹什麼?
A: 我們全家會一起吃頓大餐。
B: 你們都吃什麼?
A: 我們吃火雞，添在火雞中的餡，草莓醬，土豆泥，（馬鈴薯泥）還吃甜食南瓜餅。
B: 噢，聽起來很有意思。
A: 你想來嗎?
B: 好啊。

對話解釋

I´ll go to my grandmother´s house. 我去我奶奶家。I´ll 是I will 的縮寫。Grandmother´s house. 「´s」是表示誰…的 「´ 」是個省略號。Dinner 是

正餐或晚餐。那麼「big dinner」的意思就是很大的餐，大餐一般都有許多不同種類的肉，菜和飯等等。

Thanksgiving 感恩節是每年十一月的第四個星期四。1602 年第一批清教徒從歐洲搭五月花號船，抵達了現在的麻塞諸塞州，第一年冬天他們因為沒有食物吃，有一半以上的人都餓死了，隔年春天，當地的原住民教導他們種玉米和捕魚、打獵，經過辛勤的耕種，秋天一到玉米大豐收，有了足夠的糧食過冬。他們歡樂慶祝豐收，除了感謝上帝賜給他們一年衣食無虞，也邀請原住民朋友一起來慶祝，這就是第一個感恩節。從那時起，每年的感恩節，家人都會團聚在一起吃火雞大餐。

練習

I. 把下面的句子變成一般將來時態，用 will 加原型動詞

1) He goes to work. He will go to work.
2) John read his book.
3) We eat potato chips.
4) I am watching TV.
5) Mary has a car.

第四十課 美國的節假日（二） Holidays（II）

對話（一）

A: Hello, Lee Ren De.

B: Hi, Ding Hui.

A: You know, Christmas is coming soon.

B: Yes, I know.

A: What are you going to give your family?

B: I´m going to give my father a new watch.

A: Oh, really?

B: I´m going to give my mother a painting.

A: What will you give your brother and sister?

B: I´m going to give my brother a CD.

A: And your sister?

B: I´ll buy my sister a new dress.

對話翻譯

A: 李仁德，你好。
B: 丁慧，你好。
A: 你知道嘛，聖誕節就快到了。
B: 我知道。
A: 你要給你們家人什麼?
B: 我要給我爸爸一個新錶。
A: 我要給我媽媽一張畫。
B: 你給你兄弟姐妹什麼?
A: 我給我弟弟/哥哥一張光盤。
B: 噢，是嗎?
A: 你妹妹/姐姐呢?
B: 我要給她買件新連衣裙。

生詞

Christmas 聖誕節
soon 很快
give 給
new 新的
watch 錶
painting 油畫。
CD 音樂光盤，compact disk 的縮寫
dress 連衣裙

對話解釋

「Christmas」聖誕節，是美國最大的一個節日。每年的十二月二十五日是聖誕節。西方人在這個節日裡都要給朋友們和親屬們買禮物。許多人在聖誕節那天去教堂，因為聖誕節對基督徒來說是慶祝耶穌基督誕生的節日。You know, Christmas is coming soon. 這句話很像個問句，但說出來是個陳述句。「You know」是do you know 的簡單說法。「Christmas is coming soon.」是個陳述句。這句話的意思是你知道嘛，聖誕節就快到了。

語法

一般將來時態（二）

一般將來時態有兩種表達方法。一種表達方法是：
主語 ＋ will ＋動詞原型
例子：

I will drink tea.　我要喝茶。
Next week, Mike will visit his friend.　下週麥克要去拜訪他的朋友。
Tomorrow, we´ll see a movie.　明天我們要看個電影。
On Saturday, they´ll go to the park.　禮拜六他們將去公園。

第二種表達將來式的方法是：

主語 ＋be ＋going to ＋動詞原型

例子：

I´m going to drink tea. 我要喝茶。
Next week, Mike is going to visit his friend. 下週麥克要去拜訪他的朋友。
Tomorrow, we are going to see a movie. 明天我們要看個電影。
On Saturday, they are going to go to the park. 禮拜六我們將去公園。

這兩種將來式的構成方法有時的用法是一樣的。有時是有區別的。如果是一件馬上就要發生的事，用 to be going to 的時候多一些。比如：

That tree is going to fall down. 那棵樹要倒了（這說明那棵樹馬上就要倒了）。
That tree will fall down. 那棵樹要倒了（這是說那棵樹早晚有一天要倒）。

對話（二）

A: Hello, Ding Hui.
B: Hi, Lee.

A: Tomorrow is Saint Patrick´s Day.
B: Oh, really? What are you going to do?
A: I´m going to wear green pants and a green shirt.
B: Okay, I´ll wear green clothes, too.
A: Good. I´m also going to go to the parade.
B: May I come, too?
A: Sure.
B: Thanks. Is there anything else?
A: Yes, tomorrow, I´ll tell you a story about Leprechauns.

生詞

also 還有，還要
parade 遊行
tell 告訴
story 故事
about 關於
Leprechauns 萊珀康斯，是愛爾蘭民間傳說小老頭樣的妖精

對話翻譯

A: 你好，丁慧
B: 你好，李。
A: 明天是聖帕克里特日。

B: 哦，是嗎？ 你要幹什麼？

A: 我要穿綠色褲子和綠色襯衫。

B: 好啊，我也穿綠色的衣服。

A: 好哇，我還要去遊行。

B: 我也可以去嗎？

A: 當然。

B: 謝謝。還有別的事嗎？

A: 有，明天我要給你講一個有關小老頭樣的妖精的神話故事。

對話解釋

Is there anything else? 這是很常用的一句口語。there is 表示有，變成問句就是is there, anything 是事情，放在疑問句和否定句裡。else 是其他的。意思是還有別的事嗎？

聖帕克里特日，這是愛爾蘭國家的節日。因為美國有很多愛爾蘭人，所以美國人也慶祝這個節日。 Saint Patrick 是個牧師，住在愛爾蘭，他曾幫助過許多人。人們為了紀念他，就把三月十七日這天訂為Saint Patrick 日。在美國這個節日幾乎成了紀念愛爾蘭傳統的節日。這天人們都穿上綠色的衣服。愛爾蘭國的別名叫綠寶石島，所以人們穿綠色衣服。許多大的城市還以遊行來慶祝這個節日。除此之外，人們還吃愛爾蘭食物，喝愛爾蘭黑啤酒，講愛爾蘭故事。

練習

1. 把下面的句子變成一般將來式疑問句，用will 加原型動詞
   1) They will be here at 6 o´clock.
   2) I´ll walk to work.
   3) John eats pizza for dinner.
   4) It will snow tomorrow.
   5) She will return the book.

第四十一課 Holidays(III) 美國的節假日(三)

對話(一)

A: Hello, Ding Hui

B: Hi, Lee.

A: Tomorrow is Easter. What will we do?

B: I don´t know. What did we do last year?

A: We had an Easter Egg Hunt.

B: Oh, yes. That was fun.

A: We need a plan.

B: I´ll paint the eggs this evening.

A: That´s great.

B: Oh, no!

A: What?

B: We don´t have any eggs.

A: Don´t worry. I´ll buy some eggs after the show.

生詞

Easter 復活節
last year 去年
had have 的過去式，有，做，幹
hunt 找
Easter Egg Hunt 找復活蛋
fun 好玩， 有意思
plan 計劃
paint 把油漆塗在什麼上，油漆
after 在...以後
show 演出

對話翻譯

A: 你好，丁慧。
B: 嗨，李。
A: 明天是復活節。我們幹什麼？
B: 我不知道。我們去年幹什麼了？
A: 我們找復活雞蛋了。
B: 對了，很有意思。
A: 我們要有個計劃。
B: 我今天晚上畫雞蛋。
A: 太好了！
B: 噢，不好了！
A: 怎麼了？
B: 我們沒有雞蛋了。

A: 別著急，這個節目完了後，我就去買些雞蛋。

對話解釋

I´ll paint the eggs this evening. paint 可以是名詞也可以是動詞。當名詞講時是油漆，動詞講是把顏料、染料或油漆塗在什麼上。在我們的對話裡這個詞是動詞，我們要塗雞蛋。I´ll buy some eggs 我買些雞蛋，after the show 是做事的時間，指什麼時候李要去買雞蛋。在這裡是指我們做的英語節目。這個節目做完後，李要去商店買些雞蛋。 after 這個詞很常用。

例子：

I´ll wash the dishes after dinner. 飯後我來洗碗。
He´ll go to the store after work. 下班後他去商店。
We´ll come home after the movie. 看完電影後我們回家。

復活節經常是在每年四月份的第一個禮拜天。在西方國家裡這是一個非常大的節日。這個節日是慶祝耶穌基督復活。許多美國人那天都去教堂，有的還去餐館吃飯。那天人們還玩一個遊戲，就是Easter Egg Hunt 找復活雞蛋。是孩子們玩的遊戲。美國人把雞蛋圖上不同的顏色，藏到屋裡或房外讓孩子們找。孩子們聚在一起比賽看誰找得多。

語法複習

在這個對話裡，我們用了三個時態。有將來式，過去式和現在式。

將來式
What will we do? 我們要幹什麼?

過去式
What did we do last year? 我們去年幹什麼了？

一般現在式
We need a plan. 我們需要有個計劃。

對話（二）

A: What are you doing?
B: I´m making a picnic lunch.
A: Why?
B: I want to eat in the park today.
A: What is happening there?
B: There will be fireworks in the park tonight.
A: Oh, really?
B: Yes, today is the 4th of July.

A: Is this the American Independence Day?
B: That's right.
A: Interesting.
B: Do you want to come?
A: Sure.
B: Okay, I'll make another sandwich.

生詞

picnic 野餐
lunch 午餐
picnic lunch 在戶外吃的午餐
happen 發生
firework 煙火
another 另外一個
American Independence Day 美國獨立紀念日

對話翻譯

A: 你幹什麼呢？
B: 我在準備野餐的午餐。
A: 為什麼？
B: 我今天想在公園吃飯。
A: 那兒有什麼事嗎？
B: 今晚公園那放煙火。
A: 是嗎？
B: 對，今天是七月四日。

A: 是美國的獨立日嗎？
B: 對。
A: 有意思。
B: 你想來嗎？
A: 行啊。
B: 好，我再做一個三明治。

例子

What happened yesterday? 昨天發生什麼了？
What´s happening now? 發生什麼了？
What will happen tomorrow? 明天有什麼事？

Independence Day 獨立日。這是美國的國慶節，是每年的七月四日。美國人也把獨立日叫做「七月四日」。1776 年七月四日，美國當時的十三個州宣告從英國獨立出來。現在美國已發展成有 50 個州的國家了。美國人一般在這天都到外邊去野餐、玩。 晚間看煙火。

我們學了萬聖節，感恩節，聖誕節，聖帕克里特日，復活節，國慶節。美國有很多的節日，美國是個移民的國家，全世界不同種族的人們聚集在這裡。他們多數都慶祝他們本國傳統的節日。這也是美國這個自由的國土給人們帶來美好的一面。

練習

I. 用正確的美國節日和節日的活動搭配在一起

1) Saint Patrick's Day _____
2) Christmas ______
3) Halloween _______
4) 4th of July _______
5) Thanksgiving _______

A. We will go to a costume party and bob for apples.
B. We will wear green clothes, see a parade, and tell stories about leprechauns.
C. Everyone in the family will eat a big dinner with turkey, stuffing, and cranberry sauce.
D. We will go to the park, have a picnic, and watch the fireworks at night.
E. We will go to church, have a tree inside our house, and give presents to our family and friends.

II. 用「what」和「do」根據下面的句子問問題

1) They will see a movie. What will they do?
2) He washed his clothes yesterday.
3) Mary is an English teacher.
4) I am a doctor.
5) She is drinking tea.

III. 用英語的一般將來時態寫出你最喜歡的中國節日(這則練習有點奇怪，用將來式怎麼寫喜歡的節日呢？是不是應該用一般現在式？)

第四十二課 使用信用卡 Using a Credit Card

對話（一）

A: Do you accept credit cards?

B: Yes, we do.

A: Okay, great!

B: What would you like to have?

A: I would like that box of doughnuts, please?

B: Will that be all?

A: Yes.

B: That comes to $5.00 dollars.

A: Here is my card.

B: Just sign at the bottom.

A: Which copy do I keep?

B: You keep the yellow copy.

A: Thank you.

B: You´re welcome. Have a nice day.

生詞

accept 接受
credit 信譽，信用
card 卡
credit card 信用卡
box 盒子
a box of 一盒，是個量詞
doughnuts 油炸麵包圈，是一種食品
which 哪個
copy 副本，副印件
keep 保留，留著

對話翻譯

A: 你收信用卡嗎？
B: 對，收。
A: 那太好了！
B: 你想買什麼？
A: 我想買那盒油炸麵包圈。
B: 就要那些嗎？
A: 對。
B: 一共五塊錢。
A: 這是我的卡。
B: 請在底下簽字。
A: 我留哪頁紙？
B: 你留黃色的那頁。

A: 謝謝。

B: 不客氣。祝你一天過得愉快。

對話解釋

「doughnut」是一種食品，意思是油炸麵包圈。美國人喜歡早餐時吃 doughnuts, 喝咖啡。有的辦公室的老闆有時給僱員買doughnuts當早餐，或在開大會時，也有 doughnuts 吃。Will that be all? Will 表示將來時態，that 指那些買的東西，be 表示是，all 是所有的。問句把will 放在前面。這句話的意思是「就那些嗎」?

對話(二)

A: How are you today?

B: I´m fine, thank you. How are you?

A: Pretty good.

B: I´d like to buy these items.

A: Okay. That comes to $26.50. Will that be cash or charge?

B: Charge.

A: May I see your card?

B: Sure.

A: Here you are. Please sign at the bottom.

B: Okay.

A: You keep the yellow copy.

B: Thank you.
A: You're welcome. Have a nice day.

生詞

charge 信用卡，credit card 的另一種說法

對話翻譯

A: 你今天好嗎？
B: 我很好，謝謝。你好嗎？
A: 很好。
B: 我想買這些東西。
A: 好，一共是 $26.50 。你想付現金還是信用卡？
B: 信用卡。
A: 我可以看看你的卡嗎？
B: 當然。
A: 給你。請在這底下簽字。
B: 好。
A: 你留著黃色的收據。
B: 謝謝。
A: 不客氣。祝你有個愉快的一天。

對話解釋

Will that be cash or charge? 是現金還是信用卡？ or 在一句話裡有兩種以上的選擇時用這個字。

例如：

Do you want coffee or tea? 你想喝咖啡還是喝茶？
Are you American or English? 你是美國人還是英國人？
May I see your card? May 可以，這個字用在問話裡時是個很有禮貌的字。
may 和 please 用在一起就更有禮貌。我們知道這個意思就行了，不用翻譯出來。

例如：

May I please have some more tea？ 我可以再要點茶嗎？
May I please be excused？ 我離開可以嗎？
May I please stop？ 我可以停下來嗎？

在美國使用信用卡買東西很方便，你使用的時候一定要注意，不要隨便把你的信用卡號給別人。如果你把卡丟了，應該馬上給信用卡公司打電話，報遺失，把卡取消了。如果有人已經用了你的卡買東西了，你可以不交錢， 因為你沒有簽字。信用卡公司會酌情處理的。

練習

I. 把下面的句子譯成漢語

1) Does this store accept credit cards?
2) I'll buy that shirt with a credit card.
3) Do you want to eat fish or chicken?
4) Which color do you like?
5) These items cost 42 dollars.

第四十三課 訂飛機票 Buying Airline Tickets

對話

A: Safe and Fast Airlines, How may I help you?

B: Yes, I would like a round trip ticket to Beijing, China.

A: From which city are you flying?

B: I´d like to fly from New York.

A: When do you want to depart?

B: I´ll depart on November 7th.

A: When would you like to return?

B: I want to return on December 15th.

A: Do you want first class, business class, or economy class?

B: Economy class, please.

A: Okay, the fare for these flights is $840 dollars.

B: No problem.

A: How would you like to pay for that?
B: I´ll pay by credit card.
A: What is your name please?
B: My name is Lee Ren De.
A: What is your address?
B: I live on 320 Happy Street, Happy Town, New York.
A: What is your card number?
B: My number is 4324 6747 8009 6465. (卡號一般都有16個字，所以我又加了8個字)
A: Thank you. And what is the expiration date on the card?
B: The expiration date is 10/05.
A: Thank you. You are confirmed on flight # 201 leaving New York for Beijing on November 7th at 10:30 AM. You will return on flight #203 leaving Beijing for New York on December 15th at 2:45 PM.
B: That´s great.
A: We will send your ticket to you in the mail.
B: What is my confirmation number?
A: Your confirmation number is ABC112.
B: Thank you.
A: Have a nice day.

生詞

safe 安全
fast 快，快速
airlines 航空公司
Safe and Fast Airlines 安全快速航空公司
round trip 往返行程
ticket 票
fly 飛
depart 離開
return 回來
class 階級，等級
first class 一等(艙)
business class 商務艙
economy class 經濟艙
flight 航班
pay 交錢
expiration 過期
date 日期
expiration date 過期日期
confirmed 確定的
send 送，寄
mail 信，包裹
confirmation 確認
confirmation number 確認號碼

對話翻譯

A: 安全快速航空公司，我能怎麼幫你嗎？
B: 是的，我想買一張往返機票去中國北京。
A: 你從哪個城市出發？
B: 我從紐約出發。
A: 你什麼時候出發。
B: 十一月七日出發。
A: 你想什麼時候回來。
B: 我想十二月十五日回來。
A: 你想要一等艙、商務艙還是經濟艙？
B: 經濟艙。
A: 好，這種航班的票價是 840 美元。
B: 沒問題。
A: 你想怎麼付錢？
B: 我用信用卡付錢。
A: 你叫什麼名字？
B: 我叫李仁德。
A: 你的地址是什麼？
B: 我住在 320 號快樂街，快樂城，紐約。
A: 你的信用卡號碼是什麼？
B: 號碼是 4324 6747 8009 6465 。
A: 謝謝，卡上的過期日期是什麼？
B: 過期日期是 2005 年十月。
A: 謝謝，現在確定你在 11 月 7 號上午 10 點 30 分離開紐約去北京。 12 月 15 號 兩點 45 分離開北京回紐約。

B: 太好了。

A: 我們會給你寄去機票。

B: 我的確認號是什麼？

A: 你的確認號是 ABC112 。

B: 謝謝。

A: 祝你有個愉快的一天。

更多的生詞

frequent 頻繁的，經常發生的

flyer 飛行器，飛行員，乘飛機的人

Frequent Flyer 頻繁飛行(計劃)

flight attendant 空中服務員

對話解釋

如果你用電話訂購什麼東西的時候，你要告訴對方你的名字、地址、有時還包括電話號碼、信用卡號、什麼時候過期。「round trip」的意思是往返行程。飛機票有兩種，一種是往返機票，一種是單程機票。飛機票的價格浮動很大，有時往返機票比單程機票還要便宜。ticket 是票的意思。這裡給大家提示一下。 在美國訂飛機票，一般要提前十四天訂才能拿到好的價錢。如果你在你要去的地方過個週末，票價有時會更便宜。你訂機票的時候，對方會給你一個確認號，所以你萬一把票丟了或出了什麼問題，你可以把這個確認號告訴航空公司的服務人員，他們會給你一張新票或給你改票。

Frequent Flyer 可翻譯成頻繁飛行(計劃)。 如果你加入這個計劃，那麼你每次在同一個航空公司飛行時，電腦裡都會記下你飛了多少英里了。如果你積攢到一定英里數，他們就會給你一張免費機票。

練習

I. 把下面的句子譯成漢語

1) My flight departs at 8:30 in the morning.
2) I want to buy a round trip ticket.
3) How much is an economy class ticket?
4) What is the expiration date on your credit card?
5) Your confirmation number is 54783.

第四十四課 付賬單 Paying Bills

對話(一)

A: Hello, Ding Hui.
B: Hi, Lee Ren De.
A: Did the mail come yet?
B: Yes, it did.
A: Are there any letters for me?
B: Only bills.
A: Oh, really? What bills?
B: Here is your telephone bill and here is your electricity bill.
A: Okay. I´ll pay them tomorrow.

生詞

mail 郵件(這個字沒有複數的形式)

yet 至今，到此時 （這個字一般放在疑問句或否定句句子的後面 ）

letter 信

for 這是個介詞，表示所有權，為了...

for me 我的

only 只，僅僅

pay 交錢

them 他們，這些，那些(這個詞在句子裡做賓語)

對話翻譯

A：丁慧，你好。

B：李仁德，你好。

A：信來了嗎？

B：來了。

A：有我的信嗎？

B：只有賬單。

A：是嗎？什麼賬單？

B：這是你的電話賬單，這是你的電費賬單。

A：好，我明天交錢。

對話解釋

「mail」 郵件， 請注意這個字沒有複數的形式。Did the mail come yet?「yet」至今，到此時，這個字一般放在疑問句或否定句的後面。

對話（二）

A: What are you doing?
B: I´m writing a check.
A: Oh, really? What for?
B: I need to pay my telephone bill.
A: How much is it?
B: $82 dollars.
A: That´s expensive!
B: Yes, I know. I made many long distance calls last month.

生詞

What for? 為什麼，為什麼要做那件事
expensive 貴的
made make 的過去式
many 許多
long 長
distance 距離
long distance 長途，遠距離
long distance calls 長途電話

對話翻譯

A: 你幹什麼呢？
B: 我寫支票呢。

A: 是嗎？
B: 寫支票幹什麼？
A: 我得交電話帳單。
B: 多少錢？
A: 82 元。
B: 可真貴呀！
A: 我知道，上個月我打了很多長途電話。

英語數字

one two three four five six seven eight nine
ten 1-10
eleven twelve thirteen fourteen fifteen
sixteen seventeen eighteen nineteen 11-19
twenty 20
twenty-one twenty-two.....21, 22.....
thirty-three thirty-four.......33, 34....
forty 40
fifty 50
sixty 60
seventy 70
eighty 80
ninety 90
hundred 百
thousand 千

對話解釋

在美國最常見的賬單是電話費、電費、信用卡賬單和房租。如果你買車或房子貸款了，還要交車和房子的貸款錢。美國人多數都用支票來付賬單。

練習

1. 把支票複印三張，根據下面的內容分別寫出三張支票來（需不需要先寫一張當範例呢？）

	______________ Date
______________________________ pay to the order of	[$]
______________________________	Dollars
______________ Memo	______________ Signature

1) 瑪麗布朗Mary Brown(支票簽名得是全名)要給「Happy Telephone Company」（快樂電話公司）寫張支票，錢數是 27 dollars and 34 cents. Her telephone number is (123) 555-1234. That phone number 要寫在備忘錄 (memo)欄裡。 日期是 August 21, 2002.

2) 湯姆貝克Tom Baker要給 「Happy Electric Company」 （快樂電訊公司）寫張支票，錢數是69

dollars and 15 cents. 這是他四月份的電費。 Today's date is May 3, 2003.

3) 麥柯福特Mike Ford買電視花了 385 dollars and 50 cents. 他要給「America's best TV and Radio Store」寫張支票。 Today's date is February 24, 2004.

第四十五課 在銀行裡(一) At the Bank(I)

對話(一)

A: Hello, how are you?

B: Fine, thank you.

A: Nice to meet you.

B: Nice to meet you, too.

A: I´m Rodney.

B: Ding Hui.

A: Nice to meet you.

B: Nice to meet you, too.

A: And what brings you to First Virginia today?

B: I´d like to open an account.

A: Sure. Just have a seat and we´ll get that taken care of for you.

B: Okay.

生詞

bring 帶來
First 第一
Virginia （美國的） 佛吉尼亞州
open 開，開(門) 或打開什麼
close 關
account 帳戶
open an account 開一個帳戶
seat 座位
take care of 關照，照顧

對話翻譯

A： 嘿，你好嗎？
B： 很好， 謝謝。
A： 很高興見到你。
B： 我也很高興見到你。
A： 我是羅德尼。
B： 丁慧。
A： 很高興見到你。
B： 我也很高興見到你。
A： 你今天為什麼來佛吉尼亞第一銀行？
B： 我想開個帳戶。
A： 好啊。請坐，我們來幫你。
B： 好。

對話解釋

Just have a seat 是另外一種說法說請坐。「open」的意思是開，open an account 開個帳戶 。人們通常用把這個字用在開門或打開什麼。例子：

Please open the door. 請開門。
Please open this jar. 請把這個瓶子打開。

「open」的反義詞是「close」關。例子：

Please close the door. 請關門。
Please close this jar. 請把瓶蓋蓋上。

We'll get that taken care of for you. 這是用另一種禮貌的說法說「Yes, we'll help you」好，我們來幫你，或者是「Yes, we'll do that for you.」我們會為你做。

對話（二）

A: So you say you want to go with the basic checking account.
B: Okay.
A: And then, maybe start a savings today?
B: Okay
A: Alright.

B: So, what do you need from me?

A: All I need is your I.D..

B: Is a driver's license okay?

A: Yes, a driver's license is perfect. Okay, thank you.

生詞

so 所以
say 說
So you say 所以你是說
go 去
go with 相當於「要什麼」
basic 基本的
checking account 支票帳戶
and then 那麼就
maybe 也許，可能
start 開始
savings 儲蓄(帳戶)
perfect 很好，十全十美
monthly 每月一次
monthly fee 每個月交的錢
minimum 最低限度
balance 存款數額
minimum balance 最低限度存款數額

對話翻譯

A：所以你是說你想要個基本的支票帳戶。
B：是。
A：也許今天就開一個儲蓄帳戶？
B：行。
A：好吧。
B：那你需要我給你提供什麼？
A：我所需要的只是你的身份證。
B：駕駛執照可以嗎？
A：駕駛執照再好不過了。謝謝。

對話解釋

「So you say」所以你是說，這個經理是想要確定一下對方說的。You want to go with… 對於go這個字美國人在多種不同的地方用。多數情況下都是用在他們要跟某人到那個地方去。但在這裡經理問想要哪個帳戶。這裡的「go with」相當於「要」的意思。Basic checking account，「basic」 是基本的意思。「checking account」的意思是支票帳戶。用這個帳戶我們可以寫支票付賬單或買東西。And then, maybe start a savings today. And then 的意思是那麼就，maybe也許，可能，start 開始。這裡的「start」和「open」是一個意思， savings 在這裡是儲蓄帳戶的意思。一般這樣的帳戶存的錢有利息。

語法

詞組

英語中有許多詞組。 詞組是由兩個字以上組成的。一個可以是動詞、代詞或名詞再加個介詞或副詞組成。有的多數的詞在詞組都能保持原來的意思，有的詞在和別的字組成詞組時的意思就徹底變了。

例如：

go with, take care of, and then, what for

練習

I. 用完整的句子回答前面的問題

1) Which bank did Ding Hui go to?

2) What was the bank manager´s name?

3) Why did Ding Hui go to the bank?

4) What did the bank manager need?

5) What did Ding Hui give the bank manager?

第四十六課 在銀行裡(二) At the Bank(II)

對話(一)

A: What we'll do now is just do a credit check. Pull up your credit to make sure everything is fine, before we can open the account.

B: Okay.

A: Okay, I've checked your credit and everything is fine. So we can go ahead and open the account.

B: What information do you need?

A: Oh, I have everything on the driver's license.

B: Okay.

A: So we'll start with the basic checking account. Once you get the direct deposit, you can change your account without changing your account number. We'll just change

the type of account you have.
B: That´s good.

生詞

credit 信譽
check 檢查
credit check 檢查信譽
pull 拉，扯
pull up 拿出來，調出來
information 信息
direct 直接
deposit 存錢
direct deposit 僱主把僱員掙的工資直接存到僱員銀行的帳戶裡
once 一旦
change 改變
without 沒有，不用
account number 帳號
type 種類

對話翻譯

A：在我們給你開帳戶之前，我們要做一下信譽檢查，把你的信譽調出來，看看是不是沒什麼事。
B：好吧。
A：好，我檢查了你的信譽，沒什麼問題，所以我們可以開帳戶了。

B：你需要我的什麼資料嗎?

A：噢，我需要的都在你的駕駛執照上呢。

B：那好。

A：那麼我們就從基本的支票帳戶開始吧。一旦你有了直接儲蓄，你就可以改一下你的帳戶而不改帳號。我們只改你帳戶的種類就行了。

B：那好啊。

對話解釋

credit check，credit信譽，check檢查。兩個字加在一起就是檢查信譽的意思。銀行經理要把顧客的名字打到電腦裡查一查這個顧客以前有沒有欠的債或者有沒有沒按時付的賬單，如果有這些不好的記錄的話，銀行也許會不給開帳戶。所以有個好的信譽在美國很重要。如果你是剛來美國，沒有信譽也不要緊，有足夠的證明信也可以。Pull up your credit. pull的意思是拉，扯，pull up在這裡是拿出來，調出來的意思。這個詞組有些過時了，在沒用電腦以前，人們通常用「pull」這個字表示把檔案拿出來，這句話的意思是經理要在電腦裡查顧客的信譽。direct deposit是僱主把僱員掙的工資直接存到僱員的銀行帳戶裡。這樣做給僱員節省了每兩個星期去一次銀行的時間。Once you get the direct deposit, you can change your account without changing your account number. 這是一個條件句，在某種條件下你才能做什麼，或什麼事情才能發生。Once you get the direct deposit，once這個字是從 one變化來的。意思是一旦怎麼樣，這是先決條件。一旦你有了直接儲蓄，you can change your account 這是接下來的部份，意思是你就可以改一下你的帳戶。without changing your account number. 這是這句話的最後一部，意思是而不改帳號。

對話（二）

A: Catherine, can you give me a signature card. Okay and this is our signature card.

B: I sign?

A: You sign right on number one there. And this is your account opening card. That pen doesn´t work? Let me get you a pen that works. Here you go. Perfect. And then I need your signature again. I need your signature right here and the computer will image your signature inside the screen so we can check to make sure that is your signature.

B: Oh, really?

A: And this is for our ATM card. I just need your signature right at the bottom there. And your ATM card will arrive in approximately two weeks.

生詞

computer 電腦
image 使...成像
signature 簽字
inside 在...裡面
screen 屏幕
ATM 取錢機
ATM card 取錢卡
arrive 到達
approximately 大約

對話翻譯

A: 凱薩琳，給我一個簽字的卡。好，這是簽字卡。

B: 要我簽字?

A: 你第一個字簽在這兒，這是你的開戶卡。 那支筆不好使? 我給你一個好使的筆。給你。太好了。下面我需要你再簽一下名。在這簽名，簽名的目的是我們可以把你的簽字輸到電腦裡，所以以後我們可以檢查你的簽字是否是真的。

B: 噢，是嗎?

A: 這是我們銀行的取錢卡的申請。我需要你在這個卡的底下簽字。兩個星期左右你能收到取錢卡。

對話解釋

The computer will image your signature inside the screen. 顧客在這張卡上簽字後，銀行的工作人員把簽的字輸到電腦裡，所以以後銀行的工作人員就會辨別出簽字的支票是不是顧客簽的。這樣做對顧客的帳戶有保護作用。

練習

I. 用下面的詞造句

1) Account
2) ATM
3) Direct Deposit
4) Credit Check
5) Signature Card

第四十七課 在銀行裡(三) At the Bank(III)

對話(一)

A: And how much money do you want to deposit into your checking and savings today?

B: Let me see how much money I have. How about five hundred dollars?

A: Okay, and you want to put some in your savings account as well?

B: Can I do that?

A: Sure.

B: Okay.

A: We can put three hundred in your savings and two hundred in your checking. Is that okay?

B: Okay, sure.

A: Alright, I'll just take the money up to the

tellers. And there is your I.D. back. And I'll be right back with your receipt.

B: Okay, thank you.

生詞和詞組

teller 銀行的出納員
right back 馬上回來
receipt 收據

對話翻譯

A：你想在你的支票帳戶和儲蓄帳戶裡存多少錢?
B：我看看我有多少錢。五百元怎麼樣?
A：好，你也想在你的儲蓄帳戶裡存些錢嗎?
B：我可以那樣做嗎?
A：當然了。
B：好。
A：我們可以在你的儲蓄帳戶裡存三百元，在你的支票帳戶裡存兩百元。行嗎?
B：當然可以。
A：好，我把錢拿給出納員。這是你的駕駛執照，還給你。我馬上就會把你的收據拿來。
B：好，謝謝。

對話解釋

「teller」是銀行的出納員，也就是站在銀行櫃檯後的服務人員。I´ll be right back. 我馬上就回來。「receipt」是收據的意思。大家注意這裡的P不發音。在這裡我們給大家提一個建議，如果你在銀行裡有存款，最好在家裡設一個檔案，把銀行寄來的報告單都放在檔案裡，以便將來萬一出問題時有個憑據。

對話(二)

A: Okay, and here are your receipts. This is your receipt for the checking account. That´s two hundred dollars in your checking account today. And here´s three hundred dollars put into your savings account today.

B: Okay.

A: Here is everything. Here is all your account packet. Here is everything we talked about. Your checking and savings account, your ATM card, and also your checks, and also your first value membership. And if you have any questions, this is my card. I´m the manager here.

B: Can I call you?

A: Definitely you can call me if you have any questions regarding your account and I´ll be glad to answer them for you. Is there anything else I can do for you today?

B: No.

A: Alright, well, it was nice meeting you.

B: Nice meeting you.

A: And thank you for choosing First Virginia.

B: Thank you very much.

A: Alright.

B: Bye-bye.

A: You have a good day.

B: You, too. Bye-bye.

A: Thank you.

生詞

packet 小包裹，一打文件
account packet 帳戶的文件
value 值，價值
membership 會員
question 問題
definitely 當然地，肯定地，無疑地
regarding 關於
glad 高興
answer 回答
choose 選擇

對話翻譯

A：好，這是你的收據。這是你支票帳戶的收據，那是你今天存到支票帳戶裡的兩百元，這是你今天存到儲蓄帳戶裡的三百元。

B：好。

A：所有的都在這呢，這是你的帳戶資料，這是我們剛才說的，你的支票和儲蓄帳戶、你的取錢卡、還有你的支票、還有你的一級會員證。如果你有什麼問題，這是我的名片。我是這裡的經理。

B：我可以給你打電話嗎?

A：如果你對你的帳戶有什麼問題，你當然可以給我打電話，我會很高興地為你回答問題。今天我還能為你再做點什麼嗎?

B：不用了。

A：好，見到你很高興。

B：見到你也很高興。

A：謝謝你選擇第一維吉尼亞銀行。

B：非常感謝你。

A：好。

B：再見

A：祝你有個愉快的一天。

B：你也一樣，再見。

A：謝謝。

對話解釋

And thank you for choosing First Virginia. 為了什麼事情而謝謝別人thank you 後面用for這個詞，for 後面接的動詞要加 ing 。例如：

Thank you for helping me. 謝謝你幫助我。
Thank you for calling. 謝謝你給我打電話。

練習

I. 閱讀下面的短文，回答問題。

John deposits his money at First National Bank. He has three thousand dollars in his savings account and five hundred dollars in his checking account. The savings account is free. The checking account is also free, but John must keep a minimum balance of four hundred and fifty dollars. If his checking account is less than four hundred fifty, he will have to pay ten dollars a month. John is happy with First National Bank. The manager is very nice. The bank gave him an ATM card. John doesn´t have a credit card. He likes to pay cash for everything he needs.

1)What is the name of John´s bank?

2) How much money is in John´s savings account?
3) What is the minimum balance for John´s checking account?
4) Does John have a credit card?
5) How much does John have to pay if his checking account is less than the minimum balance?

第四十八課 電腦和互聯網(一)
Computers & Internet (I)

對話(一)

A: Can you help me?
B: Sure.
A: I need to type a report for work.
B: Let´s use the computer.
A: Okay.
B: You turn it on.
A: Yes.
B: Click on the word start at the bottom with the mouse.
A: Okay.
B: Go to programs?
A: Yes.
B: Now, click on "Microsoft Word".
A: Great, thanks.
B: You´re welcome.

生詞

type 打字
report 報告
use 使用
turn 轉動，旋轉
turn on 打開
turn off 關閉
click 按一下按鈕
start 開始，但在這裡的Start是電腦上的一個按鍵
at 表示在某處
bottom 底下，底
at the bottom 在底下
program 程序，程序表或方案，計劃
Microsoft 微軟公司，一個公司的名字
word 字
Microsoft Word 微軟公司出品的一套專門做文書處理的軟件

對話翻譯

A： 你能幫我嗎?
B： 當然了。
A： 我得寫個工作報告。
B： 我們用電腦吧。
A： 好。
B： 你把電腦打開。

A： 好。
B： 用鼠標器點一下 「Start」。
A： 好。
B： 到程序「program」 那去。
A： 好。
B： 再點微軟 Word
A： 太好了，謝謝。
B： 不客氣。

對話(二)

A: Don´t forget to save your report.
B: How do you save?
A: You can save your report by clicking on that picture of a disk with your mouse.
B: Wow! Thank you.
A: You´re welcome.
B: Hey, Lee.
A: Yes?
B: Can you please help me with one more thing?
A: Sure.
B: Can you check my report to see if I made any grammar mistakes?
A: No problem.
B: After that, we can print.

生詞

forget 忘記
save 儲存，保留
picture 圖片，照片
disk 軟盤
more 更多，更大
thing 東西，事情
one more thing 還有一件事
grammar 語法
mistakes 錯誤
after 以後
print 打印

對話翻譯

A: 別忘了把報告存起來。
B: 你怎麼存哪?
A: 你可以用鼠標點那個磁盤的小照片就把報告存起來了。
B: 哇! 謝謝。
A: 不客氣。
B: 嘿，李。
A: 幹什麼?
B: 你能再幫我做一件事嗎?
A: 當然了。
B: 你能幫看看我寫的報告有沒有語法上的錯誤嗎?

A: 沒問題。

B: 看完後我們就可以打印了。

練習

I. 用下面的詞造句

1) Report
2) Programs
3) Save
4) Mouse
5) Computer

第四十九課 電腦和互聯網(二) Computers & Internet(II)

對話 (一)

A: I need to learn more English.

B: Try the Internet.

A: Why?

B: The Internet has lots of websites with English learning programs.

A: Oh, really? Which website do you recommend?

B: Go to New Tang Dynasty TV´s website. The「Hello」show has some material there for you to learn English.

A: What´s the address?

B: http://www.ntdtv.com

A: Great! Thanks.

B: No problem.

A: Can you help me with one more thing?
B: Sure.
A: How do I log onto the Internet?

生詞

try 試試
internet 因特網，互聯網
website 網址，網站
wide 寬
World Wide 世界範圍
World Wide Web 世界範圍的網，縮寫是 WWW
which 哪個
recommend 建議
material 材料
log 把航海的行程記入日誌裡
onto 到...上
log onto 上網和其它的電腦聯結
log off 下網

對話翻譯

A ： 我得多學點英語。
B ： 試試互聯網。
A ： 為什麼?
B ： 互聯網裡有許多教英語的節目。
A ： 噢，是嗎? 你建議我上那個網站?

B：去新唐人網站，「你好」這個節目有你學英語的一些材料。

A：地址是什麼?

B：www. ntdtv. com

A：太好了。

B：沒問題。

A：你還能再幫我一個忙嗎?

B：當然。

A：我怎麼上網?

對話解釋

Internet 因特網或互聯網，這也是專門為電腦創出的新詞。這是個複合詞。net 網是漁民打魚用的網，是用繩子織起來的。inter 是互相的，互交的。互聯網就是世界上所有的電腦通過電話線或電腦電纜如DSL，都聯在一起。就好像是一個大網把整個世界給聯上了。

World Wide Web, Wide 是寬的意思 World Wide 就是世界範圍，那麼World Wide Web 直譯就是世界範圍的網，縮寫是WWW。如果哪個公司，組織或個人要想把他們的信息讓別人知道，就設計一個網站放到internet 上，每個網站都有個網址。網址多數由www開始。也就是World Wide Web的意思。

log onto 這個詞組一般是上網時用的。互聯網一般要交費用，上網時都有一個特殊的網址。 log 這個字的意思是把航海的行程記入日誌裡。onto是表示地點的詞。 那麼 log onto 就是你要上網和其它的電腦聯在一起，把你的電腦在因特網上登記成為因特網的一部份。下網是 log off 。

對話(二)

B: To log onto the Internet we need a special program.
A: Which program?
B: This computer has Explorer. We'll use this one.
A: Okay, what do I do?
B: Click on explorer.
A: Okay.
B: Now type in your password.
A: I will, but don't look.
B: Why?
A: My password is a secret.
B: No problem.
A: Okay, we're ready.
B: Now click on the top box, and type, then press Enter.
A: Great! We're here.
B: This website is in Chinese, so I think you will understand it.

生詞

special 特殊
explorer 探險者，探究者，在這裡是個軟件的名字
password 密碼，暗號
secret 秘密
top 頂上
box 方形或巨型的分格間，盒子
enter 進入，這是電腦鍵盤上的一個鍵

對話翻譯

B：上網需要一個特殊的軟件。
A：哪個軟件?
B：這個電腦裡有探險者。我們就用這個。
A：好，我得怎麼做?
B：點探險者。
A：好。
B：打你的密碼。
A：我會的，但別看。
B：為什麼?
A：我的密碼是秘密。
B：沒問題。
A：好，我們準備好了。
B：現在點上邊的方塊，打字，然後按進入。
A：太好了！我們到這來了。
B：這是個中文的網址，所以我想你能看得懂。

對話解釋

Explorer 是個軟件的名字，意思是探險者，探究者。這個字是從explore 變來的。 password 這個詞是個很舊的詞。我們可以把這個詞分開來講。 pass 是通過、穿越的意思。word 是詞、簡短的談話的意思。那麼 password就是你在通過哪個地方的時候要用的詞，也就是密碼，暗號。你說出這個暗號，把門的就會讓你過去。電腦設 password 也是為了安全起見。Enter 進入，這是你電腦鍵盤上的一個鍵。你把字打到電腦上讓電腦接收信息的時候，就按Enter，你想要的內容就顯示在電腦上了。

練習

I. 閱讀下面的短文，用完整的句子回答問題。

Tom just bought a new computer. His computer has the Internet Explorer program. Tom likes to search the World Wide Web. Tom has a dog. The dog´s name is Rex. Tom uses his dog´s name for his password. No one else knows Tom´s password. It´s a secret. Tom wants to learn Chinese. Everyday he reads Chinese language websites. It is difficult to learn a new language. Tom must practice everyday. He wants to make some Chinese friends so he can speak to them. Tom is planning to go to China next year.

Hopefully his language skills will be good enough for the trip.

1) Which language does Tom want to learn?
2) What is Tom's password?
3) What does Tom like to do?
4) When is Tom planning to go to China?
5) How does he learn Chinese?

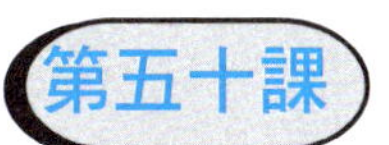

工作中的利害衝突
Conflicts in the Workplace

對話（一）

A: Hey.

B: Yes?

A: I have a problem with you.

B: I don´t like you, either.

A: What?

B: You heard me.

A: Fine! That´s the way you want it?!

B: Yes, go away!

生詞

either 也，這個字只用在否定句中，而且要放在句子的後面

heard 是hear 的過去式，聽

way 路，方式，方法

Go away! 你走，滾蛋

對話翻譯

A：嘿。

B：怎麼了?

A：我跟你有問題。(我討厭你)。

B：我也不喜歡你。

A：什麼?

B：你已經聽到我說的了。

A：好! 你就想這樣嗎?

B：對，滾蛋!

對話解釋

You heard me. 這句話的語氣很硬，意思是說，我不用再說第二遍了，你已經聽到我說的了。 That´s the way you want it?! 你想要這樣嗎，誰怕你呀。

對話（二）

A: Hey.

B: Yes?

A: I have a problem with you.

B: Oh, really? I´m sorry. How can I help you?

A: You are a bad person.

B: Wait. Please let me stop you there. What is the real issue? How can we resolve this in a positive way?

A: Well, yesterday you didn´t finish your half of the project.

B: Yes, I know.

A: What happened?

B: I had a family problem and had to go home early. I told the manager. Didn´t he tell you?

A: No, he didn´t.

B: Oh. Well I´m happy to work overtime today to finish the work.

A: I´m sorry.

B: That´s okay. This was just a misunderstanding.

A: Yes, I guess so.

生詞

person 人
wait 等一等
real 真的，真正的
issue 問題
resolve 解決
positive 正面的，積極的
finish 完成
half 一半

project 工作項目
have to 不得不，一定要
go home 回家
early 早點，早
had to go home early 不得不早點回家
told tell 的過去式，告訴
well 嗯，好啊
overtime 額外時間，加班時間，超出時間的
misunderstanding 誤解，誤會
guess 猜

對話翻譯

A：嘿。
B：怎麼了?
A：我跟你有問題。(我討厭你)。
B：是嗎?對不起。我該怎麼做呢?
A：你是個壞人。
B：等一下。請你不要繼續往下說了。到底是什麼問題?我們怎麼才能用積極的辦法解決呢?
A：昨天你連工作的一半都沒幹完。
B：對，我知道。
A：發生了什麼事?
B：我家出事了，我不得不早點回家。我告訴經理了，他沒告訴你嗎?
A：對，他沒告訴我。
B：我願意今天加班把事做完。

A : 對不起。
B : 沒關係。
A : 這是誤會了。
B : 對，我猜也是。

對話解釋

這段對話的語調是不是不一樣了？我們發現，當你的心態總是很平和的時候，有矛盾時總是找找自己哪裡不對了，矛盾很快就會解決。別管別人生氣是對與錯，只要你總是保持一顆平和的心態，只要你誠懇和善良，什麼問題都能得到圓滿的解決。

have to 不得不，一定要，這是個很常用的詞組。

例句：

I had to call my mother. 我得給我媽媽打個電話。
She had to sleep. 她得睡覺。
Children have to go to school. 孩子必須得上學。
We had to do our homework. 我們必須得做作業。
Please let me stop you there.
請讓我來阻止你，意思是說，請你不要繼續往下說了。這句話有禮貌但也很嚴厲。就是說你不想讓情況變得更壞。
How can we resolve this issue in a positive way?

我們怎麼能用積極的方式把這個問題解決了呢?

下面我們學一些怎樣用英語表達使人鎮定下來的詞和句子:

Calm down 冷靜下來

I don´t want any trouble. 我不想有麻煩。

I´m sorry. 對不起。

compassion 愛,善良,慈悲,同情

練習

I. 把下面的句子譯成漢語

1) I´m sorry.This is just a misunderstanding.
2) Please don´t be angry.
3) What happened yesterday?
4) I have a problem with her.
5) The real issue is that we must finish our work.

第五十一課 在機場裡（安全檢查）
At the Airport (Security Check)

對話（一）

A: Hello Sir. Are you checking in today?
B: Yes, I am.
A: Where are you flying to?
B: I am going to New York.
A: May I see an I.D., please?
B: No problem, here you are.
A: How many bags are you checking in today?
B: I´m checking two bags.
A: Did you pack those bags yourself sir?
B: Yes, I did.
A: Has anyone approached you or asked you to carry anything else on this flight?
B: No
A: Great. Here is your boarding pass. Please

go to gate number H23.
B: Thank you.

生詞

bag 包，行李
pack 包裝，打包
approach 接近
carry 攜帶，搬運
boarding pass 登機牌
gate 門，登機口

對話翻譯

A: 先生你好。你今天要登記嗎?
B: 對。
A: 你往哪飛?
B: 我去紐約。
A: 我可以看你的身份證嗎?
B: 沒問題，給你。
A: 你托運幾個行李?
B: 兩個。
A: 是你自己打包的行李嗎，先生?
B: 是的。
A: 有人接近你，讓你在這個飛機上帶東西嗎?
B: 沒有。
A: 好，這是你的登機牌，請去H23登機口。

B: 謝謝。

對話解釋

check 支票，檢查 。check in 是登記的意思。行李托運時，也用 check in 這個詞。給行李登記。你托運行李時會給你一個票，你要把這個票放好，萬一你的行李丟了可以根據這個票查出來你的行李在哪。pack 包裝，打包。服務員在給你托運行李的時候會問是不是你自己裝的行李，有沒有人讓你帶什麼東西上飛機。gate 門，登機口。機場的每一架飛機都停在不同的登機口旁邊。登機口一般用字母和號碼排列。你登機時，要到指定的登機口去。

對話（二）

A: May I see your ticket and photo I.D. please?
B: Sure.
A: Please put all your bags on the machine.
B: Okay.
A: Do you have any metal items like keys or coins in your pockets?
B: Yes I do. I have keys.
A: Please put them on the machine, too.
B: No problem.
A: Do you have a cell phone or pager?
B: Yes I do. I have a cell phone.

A: Please put your phone on the machine.
B: Okay.
A: Step over here, please. Hold out your arms, please. Take off your shoes, please. Thank you.
B: May I go now?
A: Yes, you are all set.
B: Thank you.

生詞

machine 機器，在對話裡是X光機。人通過這個X光機能看到包裡的東西
metal 金屬
key 鑰匙
pocket 衣袋，口袋
cell phone 手機
pager BB機
step 步行，邁步
over here 這邊
hold 在這裡表示保持一個狀態
hold out 伸出
take off 脫掉
put on 穿上
set 完事了的

對話翻譯

A: 我可以看一下你的機票和帶照片的身份證嗎?
B: 可以。
A: 請把你所有的行李都放在機器上。
B: 好。
A: 你衣服口袋裡有像鑰匙或硬幣一類的金屬物品嗎?
B: 有，我有鑰匙。
A: 請把鑰匙也放在機器上。
B: 沒問題。
A: 你有手機或 BB 機嗎?
B: 有，我有手機。
A: 請把手機放在機器上。
B: 好。
A: 請走到這邊來。請把胳膊伸平。請把鞋脫下來。謝謝。
B: 我可以走了嗎?
A: 好，你沒事了。
B: 謝謝。

對話解釋

Hold out your arms, please 請把你的胳膊伸平。You are all set 你好了，沒你的事了。Take off your shoes, please. take off 脫掉，一般指脫衣服，脫鞋等。穿衣服是 put on。安檢時，警察有時也檢查鞋，因為有的危險分子把刀或凶器藏在鞋裡。

練習

I. 用正確的答案和問題搭配在一起

1) Do you have any metal items in your pockets?
____

2) How many bags are you checking in today?
____

3) Where are you going? ______

4) Has anyone approached you or asked you to carry something? ______

5) May I see your I.D., please? ________

A) I´m going to Shanghai.

B) No, I don´t.

C) Sure, here is my passport.

D) No one has asked me anything.

E) I´m checking 4 bags.

第五十二課 與鄰居見面 Meet the Neighbors

對話（一）

A: Hello.

B: Yes, who is it?

A: My name is Lee Ren De. I´m your next door neighbor.

B: Oh, really? My name is Ding Hui.

A: Nice to meet you.

B: Nice to meet you, too.

A: I have a problem.

B: What problem?

A: I´m baking a cake for my girlfriend, but I ran out of sugar. May I please borrow a cup of sugar from you?

B: Sure.

A: Thank you so much.

B: You´re welcome.

生詞

next 下一個
door 門
next door 下一個門，也就是緊挨的鄰居
neighbor 鄰居
bake 烤
girlfriend 女朋友
run 跑，過去式ran
run out 用完了，沒有了
borrow 借，借用

對話翻譯

A: 喂。
B: 唉，是誰呀?
A: 我叫李仁德，我是緊挨著你家的鄰居。
B: 是嗎? 我叫丁慧。
A: 很高興見到你。
B: 我也很高興見到你。
A: 我有點麻煩。
B: 什麼麻煩?
A: 我在給我的女朋友烤蛋糕，但沒有糖了。我可以你借一杯糖嗎?
B: 當然可以。
A: 太謝謝你了。
B: 不客氣。

對話解釋

ran 是run的過去式，是跑的意思。 ran out和run好像沒有什麼關係，意思是東西用完了，沒有了。在這個對話裡， A沒有糖了，沒糖就不能烤蛋糕。
borrow 的意思是借，借用，是從別人那裡借來。如借給別人什麼東西是用另外一個字 lend 。

對話（二）

A: Hi, I´m Lee Ren De.
B: Ding Hui.
A: I´m your neighbor down the street.
B: Okay.
A: My son is your son´s friend at school.
B: Oh, yeah!
A: My boy would like to invite your son over to our house tonight for a sleepover.
B: No problem. What time should he come over?
A: How about 7 o´clock?
B: That´s great. Should he have dinner first?
A: No, that´s okay. I think the boys want to order pizza.
B: When should I pick my son up?
A: Don´t worry. I´ll bring him home after lunch tomorrow.
B: Great.

A: Good-bye.

B: Good-bye.

A: Oh! I forgot one more thing.

B: What´s that?

A: Are you going to the school play next week?

B: Yes, I am.

A: Maybe we can carpool.

B: That would be great.

生詞

down 在...下面

street 街道

invite 邀請

tonight 今天晚上

sleepover 過夜，這是專門描寫小孩想在他們的朋友家過夜的詞

should 應該

think 想，認為

order 訂，訂貨

pick up (用車)接

bring 帶來

after 在...以

lunch 午飯，午餐

play 話劇，打球，踢球，玩

school play 學校學生演的話劇

carpool 輪流出車，集體乘坐

對話翻譯

A: 嗨，我是李仁德。
B: 丁慧。
A: 我是街那邊你的鄰居。
B: 是嘛。
A: 在學校裡我的兒子是你的兒子的朋友。
B: 噢，是呀！
A: 我兒子想請你兒子今晚來我家過夜。
B: 沒問題。他什麼時候去?
A: 七點可以嗎?
B: 太好了，他要先吃晚飯嗎?
A: 不用了，我想他們要訂購比撒餅。
B: 我什麼時候去接我的兒子?
A: 不用擔心，明天午飯後我把他帶回家。
B: 好啊。
A: 再見。
B: 再見。
A: 噢，我忘了一件事。
B: 什麼事?
A: 下禮拜你去看學校的話劇嗎?
B: 去呀。
A: 也許我們可以一起開車去。
B: 那太好了。

對話解釋

down the street 在街道的那邊，也是在一條街上。比 next door 要遠得多。sleepover 是過夜的意思，這是專門描寫小孩想在他們的朋友家過夜的詞。I think the boys want to order pizza. 我想孩子們想訂購比撒餅。當句子裡講我想或誰想的時候，要把誰想放在前邊，後面加想什麼。例子：

He thinks it is too cold outside. 他想外面太冷了。
I think we need to buy some apples. 我想我們應該買些蘋果。
We think English is interesting. 我們認為英語有意思。

school play就是學校學生演的話劇。很多學校一年都有一次話劇演出。carpool 是輪流出車，集體乘坐的意思，如果幾個人都到一個地方去，開一輛車的話，可以省車和省汽油。有的人在一個公司工作的也 carpool，這是一個很好的省油省錢的辦法。

練習

I. 根據下面的每句話問一個問題

1) Sure you may borrow a cup of sugar.
2) No, he´s not going to the school play.
3) She should come over at 3 o´clock.
4) I need 3 eggs.
5) No problem. We can carpool to work.

第五十三課 語音（一）Phonics （I）

元音

Aa, Ee, Ii, Oo, Uu, Yy

輔音

Bb, Cc, Dd, Ff, Gg, Hh, Jj, Kk, Ll, Mm, Nn, Pp, Qq, Rr, Ss, Tt, Vv, Ww, Xx, Zz

清輔音

字母發音聲帶不動，我們把這種輔音稱為清輔音。

濁輔音

發音時聲帶顫動，也就是用聲帶發的音。我們把這種輔音稱為濁輔音。

閉止音

p b

在發這兩個音的時候，雙唇輕輕閉合，壓迫氣流，使氣流由口腔突破雙唇而出。p 是清輔音，b 是濁輔音。

panda 熊貓 ball 球

t d

take 拿 down 下

發這兩個音的時候，先將雙唇微微張開，舌尖抵住上齒齦，憋氣，然後悄悄用力將舌尖彈開。t 是清輔音，d 是濁輔音。

k g

發這兩個音的時候，雙唇微開，舌後跟往上翹起，並抵住口腔上方的軟齶部份，把氣憋住，然後將氣悄悄用力將舌彈出，使氣流從口中沖出， k 相當於漢語咳嗽的「咳」，但聲帶不振動，g 相當漢語「哥」的發音。

kite 風箏 gum 口香糖

練習

paper	紙	baseball	棒球	tomorrow	明天	dance	舞蹈
pour	倒	basket	籃子	take	拿	dessert	甜食
panda	熊貓	boy	男孩	tap	彈	down	向下
party	聚會	bottom	底	tear	眼淚	doll	娃娃
pass	通過	bunch	束	table	桌子	day	天

cat	貓	gum	口香糖
car	車	go	去
cook	廚師	get	得到

kite 風箏 gold 金子
keep 保持 good 好

摩擦音

顧名思義，摩擦音就是由牙齒和嘴唇的摩擦發出的音。摩擦音也有清輔音和濁輔音。

f v

這兩個摩擦音是由牙齒和嘴唇的摩擦發出的音。發 f 這個音時，上齒輕輕咬住下唇內側，將氣流從唇齒的縫隙輕輕吹出來，不振動聲帶。和漢語「夫」字的發音差不多。v 的發音與 f 的發音大致相同，但聲帶振動，漢語裏沒有這個發音，所以大家發這個音的時候要注意。f 是清輔音，v 是濁輔音。

fly 飛 victim 受害者

th

這個發音漢語中沒有對應的字，發音時雙唇微開，舌頭伸出來，上下齒輕輕咬住舌頭，將氣流從牙縫輕輕吹出來。 因為中文沒有這個發音，所以大家發音的時候一定要注意，別忘了把舌頭伸出來。舌頭不伸出來，這個音就發不對。 th 既是清輔音又是濁輔音。

thin 薄 this 這個

s z

這組的發音很容易，s 和漢語的「絲」字幾乎一樣，就是聲帶不振動。發此音時，上下齒輕輕閉合，向外吹氣，不振動聲帶。z 振動聲帶。s 是清輔音，z 是濁輔音。

sit　坐　　　　zipper　拉鏈

sh　s

sh 和漢語的失差不多。發此音時，雙唇翹起，向前突出，上下齒微閉，舌頭上揚，向外吹氣，不振動聲帶。s的發音和sh的發音幾乎一樣，就是聲帶振動，有點類似漢語的「日」。sh 是清輔音，s 是濁輔音。

shoe　鞋　　　　treasure　財富

在 treasure 這個字裏，s 的發音在中間。輔音的發音不限定位置，可以在詞的前邊、中間、後邊，還可以有幾個同樣的發音出現在一個詞裏。

h

h這個摩擦音，是從嗓子的後面發出來的，這是個清輔音。

happy　高興

練習

fly	飛	victim	受害者	thin	薄	the	（定冠詞）
fat	胖	vase	花瓶	thing	東西	this	這個
flower	花	victory	勝利	think	想	these	這些

sit	坐	zipper	拉鏈	shoe	鞋	treasure	財富
soup	湯	zero	零	shower	淋浴	measure	測量
simple	簡單	zoo	動物園	show	演出	pleasure	快樂

happy	高興
hand	手
help	幫助

破擦音

破擦音是由閉止音和摩擦音和在一起的音，英語裏只有兩個破擦音，其中一個是濁輔音，一個是清輔音。發音時，雙唇翹起向前突出，上下齒微閉，舌頭微微上揚，然後憋氣，用力使氣流振開，從上下齒而出發出類似「七」的短促聲音。

ch j

China 中國 joke 玩笑

練習

China	中國	joke	玩笑
church	教堂	judge	法官
chimp	黑猩猩	fudge	巧克力甜點
child	孩子	jump	跳
choose	選擇	Japan	日本

鼻音

顧名思義，鼻音就是用鼻子發出的音。 所有的鼻音都是濁輔音。發音時，聲帶要振動。

m　　n

m的發音很簡單，發此音時，雙唇閉合，舌頭平放，振動聲帶，氣流由鼻腔出來，發出的聲音就像我們閉著嘴巴發「嗯」的鼻音。

發n音時，雙唇微張，舌尖向上，輕輕抵住上齒齦，振動聲帶，氣流由鼻腔出來，發出的聲音就像我們張嘴發「嗯」的鼻音。

Monday 星期一　　ring 圈

練習

Monday	星期一	neat	整齊	ring	圈
man	男人	none	沒有任何東西	sing	唱歌
many	許多	no	不	king	國王
month	月	nap	午睡	bang	砰
master	主人	nose	鼻子	song	歌

邊音

l

發這個音的時候雙唇要張大一些，舌尖向上，抵住上齒齦，振動聲帶，氣流由舌頭兩側出來。L音類似我們發漢語「了」之前，舌頭翹起振動聲帶的聲音。

lake 湖

練習

Lee 李
leap 跳躍
love 愛
lap 膝
library 圖書館

振動音

r

振動音也叫捲舌音。發振動音時，顧名思義，舌頭要在口腔裏振動，才能發出這個音來。英語裏只有一個振動音，但有幾種發音。發這個音時，舌頭要向上捲。

rain 雨　star 星星　teacher 老師

練習

rain	雨	bar	酒吧	teacher	老師
ripe	熟	star	星星	baker	麵包師
reach	達到	or	或者	better	比較好
read	讀	war	戰爭	terrible	可怕的

半元音

半元音發音時很像元音但又不是元音。這個音在詞裏的位置更像輔音。這兩個半輔音都是濁輔音。聲帶要振動。

w

發此音時雙唇向前突出，振動聲帶就行了。很像漢語裏烏鴉的「烏」的發音。

water 水

y

發這個音時，舌頭向下，音是從舌後發出來的。

練習

water	水	yes	是
willow	柳樹	you	你
whip	鞭子	yoke	軛
wash	洗	yellow	黃色
Wednesday	星期三	yak	犁牛

音的搭配

有些輔音常在一起搭配。在兩個輔音搭配的時候，發音時聽起來像一個輔音。

b 和 r 的搭配

brush	刷子	bread	麵包
brook	溪流	break	毀壞

t 和 r 的搭配

trip	旅行	trade	貿易
train	火車	track	軌跡

p 和 l 的搭配

plate	盤子	plane	平面
play	玩	plant	植物

c 和 k 的搭配

crack	敲碎	track	軌跡
sack	包	pack	包裝

有的輔音和另一個輔音在一起不發音。這點大家得注意。

know	知道	knew	知道
gnome	格言	gnu	牛羚
which	哪個	whip	鞭子
thought	思想	bought	買

第五十四課 語音（二）Phonics (II)

元音

長元音

長元音發音時和字母本身的發音是一樣的。

Aa, Ee, Ii, Oo, Uu

如果一個詞裏有一個輔音後面接元音然後接輔音，結尾是E －
輔音 + 元音 + 輔音 +E ，其中的元音發音和字母一樣，也就是長元音。

A	take	拿	I	kite	風箏
	mate	夥伴		line	線
	sale	賣		wipe	擦
O	note	筆記	U	brute	野獸
	mole	黑痣		flute	笛子
	hole	洞		cute	逗人喜愛的

ee 在一起發的音和字母 e 的發音是一樣的

E Lee (name)

ea 也發 e 的音

E meat 肉

week 星期
feet 腳

each 每個
bean 豆子

ai 在一起發 A 的音

A wait 等
rain 雨
pain 痛

oa 在一起發 O 的音

O boat 船
road 路
float 漂浮

ie 在一起發 I 的音

I pie 餡餅
die 死

i 後面加 gh 也發 I 的音

I high 高
sigh 嘆氣
flight 航班
fight 打架

y

y 有時它是個輔音，有時是元音。下面的三個字中的 y 發長元音 I。

I sky 天空
fly 飛
try 試

y 有時也發長元音 E 的音

E candy 糖
quickly 快
happy 高興

ay 發 a 的音

A play 玩
stay 停留
today 今天

練習

take 拿	kite 風箏	note 筆記	brute 野獸	beef 牛肉
mate 夥伴	line 線	mole 黑痣	flute 笛子	week 星期
sale 賣	wipe 擦	hole 洞	cute 可愛的	feet 腳

meat 肉	wait 等	boat 船	pie 餡餅	sky 天
each 每個	rain 雨	road 路	die 死	fly 飛
bean 豆	pain 痛	float 漂浮	high 高	try 試

sigh 嘆氣	candy 糖	play 玩
flight 航班	quickly 快	stay 停留
fight 打架	happy 高興	today 今天

短元音

短元音與長元音相比，元音的的發音很短。短元音的發音規則是英語單詞的拼寫中輔音後面接元音，然後又接一個輔音，也就是輔音＋元音＋輔音，這裏的元音發短元音。

I	sit	坐	E	men	男人
	sip	啜		pen	鋼筆
	sick	生病		net	網
O	hot	熱	U	nut	堅果
	pot	鍋		pull	拉

not 不

butter 奶油

注：u 在這裏發 a 的音。

短 A 有幾種不同的發音

hat 帽子
cat 貓
pack 包裝

A 的另一個發音

father 爸爸
brother 兄弟
water 水

A 的第三個發音

all 全部
ball 球
small 小

I

I 這個字母經常和 R 在一起。

ir bird 鳥
earth 地球

練習

sit 坐	men 男人	hot 熱	nut 堅果	hat 帽子
sip 啜	pen 筆	pot 鍋	pull 拉	cat 貓
sick 生病	net 網	not 不	butter 奶油	pack 包裝

father 爸爸	all 全部	bird 鳥
bother 打擾	ball 球	earth 地球
water 水	small 小	

特殊音和例外音

oo	pool 游泳池	oi 和 oy	boy	男孩
	stool 板凳		toy	玩具
	fool 傻子		spoil	寵壞
			toil	苦工

qu這兩個字母在一起時發音更像輔音。q的發音是k，那麼u的發音像w，放在一起就是kw。

qu	quick 快	ow	how	怎麼
	quite 相當		cow	牛
	quiet 肅靜		bow	鞠躬
			flower	花

ow 在一起時也發長元音o 的音

show 演出
bow 弓

另外一個值得注意的是在輔音+元音+輔音+E，這個規律中 O 的發音，同以上的發音完全不同。

o love 愛
dove 鴿子
above 上面

a

英語中共有三個冠詞 "a" "an" 或 "the" 。我們在句子中怎麼發 a 這個音呢?如果我們說的慢，就發長元音 a 。如果我們說的快，就發短元音 a 。

This is a table.

練習

pool	游泳池	boy	男孩	quick	快	how	怎麼
stool	板凳	toy	玩具	quite	相當	cow	牛
fool	傻子	spoil	寵壞	quiet	肅靜	bow	鞠躬
		toil	苦工			flower	花

show	演出	love	愛	a	一個
bow	鞠躬	dove	鴿子		
		above	上面		

課文

Fall in America is very beautiful. The leaves on the trees change color. They become red, yellow, brown, and orange. The weather gets a little cooler. People begin to wear sweaters and jackets. I love to look out at the countryside, smell the delicious clean air, and enjoy a fall day. I can read a book outside while sitting on a pile of leaves. It is truly relaxing.

美國的秋天非常美麗，樹上的葉子變了顏色，變成紅色、黃色、褐色和桔黃色。天氣變得有點涼，人們穿上了毛衣和夾克服。我喜歡觀看外面的農村風景，呼吸著充滿清香的乾淨空氣，享受秋季的一天。坐在外面的一堆樹葉上，我讀著書。真放鬆啊。

答案 Answer Key

Lesson One

I.

1) you
2) I
3) What
4) How
5) Nice

II.

1) I am fine.
2) My name is ________.
3) Her name is Mary.

Lesson Two

I.

1) A E I O U

II.

1) a
2) a
3) an

4) a
5) an

III.

1) This is a lamp.
2) This is a book.
3) This is an apple.
4) This is a pen.
5) This is an envelope.

IV.

1) Yes, it is.
2) No, it isn't.
3) No, it isn't.
4) Yes, it is.
5) No, it isn't.

Lesson Three

I.

1) Mary's
2) Tom's
3) Lee's
4) Ding Hui's
5) Nancy's

II.

1) Your
2) My
3) His
4) Her
5) Your

Lesson Four

I.

1) apples
2) pens
3) lamps
4) envelopes
5) telephones

II.

1) These are lamps.
2) These are pens.
3) These are books.
4) These are apples.
5) These are envelopes.

Lesson Five

I.

1) have
2) has
3) have
4) has
5) have

II.

1) He has 4 hats.
2) They have 12 flowers.
3) No, she doesn't.
4) Yes, they do.
5) No, we don't.

Lesson Six

I.

1) A lamp costs $4.30.
2) No, she doesn't.
3) Pens cost $0.55.
4) Yes, they do.
5) Apples cost $0.20.

Lesson Seven

I.

1) I want an apple.
2) I want a banana.
3) I want some pens.
4) I want a lamp.
5) I want some envelopes.

II.

1) I want to go.
2) I want to eat.
3) I want to sleep.
4) I want to buy.
5) I want to drink.

Lesson Eight

I.

1) B
2) D
3) A
4) C
5) E

Lesson Nine

I.

1) This is a blue dress.
2) That is a red hat.
3) This is a green shirt.
4) These are white shoes.
5) These are yellow pants.

II.

1) I like apples.
2) John likes green peppers.
3) They like to play basketball.
4) She likes to read books.
5) I like green.

Lesson Ten

I.

1) John is from America.
2) His shoes are red.
3) He likes to drink tea.
4) He wears extra large shirts.
5) No, he isn' t. He is tall.

II. 寫一段介紹你們家裏人的小短文

Lesson Eleven

I.

1) I' m busy today.
2) Do you want to see a movie today?
3) Sure.
4) I like Sundays.
5) I like Fridays.

Lesson Twelve

I.

1) It is 7:30.
2) It is 1 o' clock.
3) It is 11:15.
4) It is 3:05.
5) It is 4:53.

II.

1) half
2) quarter
3) o' clock
4) to
5) after

Lesson Thirteen

I.

1) Tom likes to watch TV.
2) We want to wash clothes on Sunday.
3) They play basketball on Fridays.
4) Mary studies English.
5) Lee works on Saturdays.

Lesson Fourteen

I.

1) 我們去餐館吧。
2) 我們不吸煙。
3) 我需要一把叉子。
4) 你想幹什麼？
5) 你(們)需要幾份菜單？

Lesson Fifteen

I.

1) I would like to eat some soup.
2) I would like to eat some ice-cream.
3) I would like to eat a sandwich.
4) I would like to eat a salad.
5) I would like to eat some cake.

II.

1) 你想喝點茶嗎？
2) 我想看電視。
3) 他們想吃點蘋果。
4) 她想吃東西嗎？
5) 我們想去跳舞。

Lesson Sixteen

I.

1) am
2) is
3) are
4) is
5) are

II.

1) She is a student.
2) They are police officers.
3) I am a ________.
4) He is a baker.
5) Mary is a secretary.

Lesson Seventeen

I.

1) on
2) between
3) under
4) next to
5) in

Lesson Eighteen

I.

1) I' d
2) You' d
3) He' d
4) She' d
5) They' d
6) We' d

II.

1) I' d like to go to the library.
2) He' d like to go to the post office.
3) They' d like to go to the movie theatre.
4) We' d like to go to the park.
5) She' d like to go to the bank.

Lesson Nineteen

I.

1) 銀行在超級市場和電 影院中間。
2) 往後走。
3) 學校在快樂大道上。
4) 向左轉。
5) 向前一直走三條街。

Lesson Twenty

I.

1) Speed Limit
2) Stop
3) Do Not Enter
4) No Parking
5) Exit

Lesson Twenty One

I. Fill in Application.

Lesson Twenty Two

I.

1) I'm going downtown.
2) They are studying English.
3) We are playing basketball.
4) I'm eating pizza.
5) She is drinking tea.
6) Tom is reading a book.
7) You are writing an application.
8) My friend is sleeping.

Lesson Twenty Three

I.

1) I am writing letters.
2) He is returning a book.
3) They are making phone calls.
4) Mary is meditating.
5) Lee is buying some stamps.

Lesson Twenty Four

I.

1) Mary likes to buy clothes.

2) Every Saturday she goes to the clothing store.
3) The clothing store is downtown.
4) The bus fare is $1.50 each way.
5) The bus comes to the stop exactly at 8:30 in the morning.

Lesson Twenty Five

I.

1) It is sunny today.
2) It is cloudy today.
3) It is windy today.
4) It is rainy today.
   It is raining.
5) It is snowy today.
   It is snowing.

Lesson Twenty Six

I.

1) Mary feels happy.
2) I feel sick.
3) Tom feels worried.
4) We feel sad.

5) She feels calm.

II.

1) 我胃疼。
2) 我膝蓋疼。
3) 他耳朵疼。
4) 她手疼。
5) 湯姆頭疼。

Lesson Twenty Seven

I.

1) E
2) A
3) D
4) B
5) C

Lesson Twenty Eight

I.

1) My friend is injured.
2) She is bleeding.
3) My house is on fire.
4) I need an ambulance.

5) He has a broken leg.

Lesson Twenty Nine

I.

1) B
2) E
3) C
4) D
5) A

Lesson Thirty

I.

1) She is a doctor in the city hospital.
2) Andy is John' s father.
3) Andy likes to play chess in the park.
4) No, he doesn' t.
5) He is 9 years old.

Lesson Thirty One

I.

1) played

2) went
3) watched
4) was
5) ate

Lesson Thirty Two

I.

1) C
2) E
3) B
4) D
5) A

Lesson Thirty Three

I.

1) 我正要去郵局。
2) 一共 50 美分。
3) 我的選擇是什麼？
4) 我想寄這封信給我奶奶。
5) 請用一般航空郵件寄。

Lesson Thirty Four

I.

1) If you send it by global priority, that will be $5.00.
2) If he is happy, he will smile.
3) If they are hungry, they can eat apples.
4) If you are tired, you can go to sleep.
5) If she had money, she'd buy a new dress.

II.

1) or
2) by
3) Let's
4) or
5) Let's

Lesson Thirty Five

I.

1) Would you like any phone cards or anything today?
2) Would you like an apple or an orange?
3) Do you want to dance or watch TV?
4) Is she happy or sad?
5) Can we play basketball or soccer?

Lesson Thirty Six

I.

1) He has a dog, horse, cow, and a pig.
2) Mary wants a house, car, and a bicycle.
3) Let's go to the park, post office, bank, and the store.
4) Her apartment has a kitchen, bedroom, and a balcony.
5) I want to eat a hamburger, salad, and some oranges.

Lesson Thirty Seven

I.

1) Water is free, but you have to pay for electricity.
2) He has an English book, but he can't find it.
3) I'm hungry, but I don't have any food.
4) I need to buy a stamp, but the post office is closed.
5) She wants to go to the movies, but she is very busy.

Lesson Thirty Eight

I.

1) The lease is for one year.
2) No, there isn't. It's free.
3) There are 4 rooms in the apartment.
4) Yes, it does.
5) The rent is $1500 a month plus utilities.

Lesson Thirty Nine

I.

1) He will go to work.
2) John will read his book.
3) We will eat potato chips.
4) I will watch TV.
5) Mary will have a car.

Lesson Forty

I.

1) They are going to be here at 6 o'clock.
2) I am going to walk to work.
3) John is going to eat pizza for dinner.
4) It is going to snow tomorrow.
5) She is going to return the book.

Lesson Forty One

I.

1) B
2) E
3) A
4) D
5) C

II.

1) What will they do?
2) What did he do yesterday?
3) What does Mary do?
4) What do you do?
5) What is she doing?

III. Free writing exercise

Lesson Forty Two

I.

1) 這間商店接受信用卡嗎？
2) 我要用信用卡買那件襯衫。
3) 你想吃魚還是雞？
4) 你喜歡哪一種顏色？
5) 這些一共 42 美元。

Lesson Forty Three

I.

1) 我的飛機在早上 8:30 起飛。
2) 我想買一張往返機票。
3) 經濟艙機票一張多少錢？
4) 你卡上的過期日期是什麼？
5) 你的確認號是 54783 。

Lesson Forty Four

I. checks

1)

08/21/2002
Date

Happy Telephone Company [$ 27.34]
pay to the order of

Twenty Seven and 34/100----------Dollars.

Bill for (123) 555-1234
Memo

Mary Smith
Signature

2)

05/03/2003
Date

Happy Electric Company [$ 69.15]
pay to the order of

Sixty Nine and 15/100--------------Dollars.

April Electric Bill
Memo

Tom Baker
Signature

3)

02/24/2004
Date

America's Best TV and Radio Store [$ 385.50]
pay to the order of

Three hundred Eighty Five and 50/100---Dollars.

Television
Memo

Michael Goodheart
Signature

Lesson Forty Five

Dialogue questions

I.

1) Ding Hui went to the First Virginia Bank.

2) The manager's name was Rodney.
3) She wanted to open an account.
4) He needed her I.D.
5) She gave him her driver's license.

Lesson Forty Six

Examples

I.

1) I'd like to open an account.
2) I need to go to the ATM.
3) May I have direct deposit?
4) I must do a credit check.
5) Here is your signature card. Please sign at the bottom.

Lesson Forty Seven

I.

1) John's bank's name is First National Bank.
2) John has three thousand dollars is his savings account.
3) The minimum balance is four hundred and fifty dollars.

4) No, he doesn' t.

5) If his checking account is less than four hundred fifty, he will have to pay ten dollars a month.

Lesson Forty Eight

Examples

I.

1) I need to write a report.
2) Do you have an Internet program?
3) Don' t forget to save you report.
4) I don' t have a mouse.
5) Your computer is nice.

Lesson Forty Nine

I.

1) Tom wants to learn Chinese.
2) Tom' s password is Rex.
3) Tom likes to search the World Wide Web.
4) Tom is planning to go to China next year.
5) He reads Chinese language websites everyday.

Lesson Fifty

I.

1) 對不起，這是個誤會。
2) 請別生氣。
3) 昨天發生了什麼事？
4) 我跟她有問題。(我討厭她)。
5) 真正的問題是我們必須把工作做完。

Lesson Fifty One

I.

1) B
2) E
3) A
4) D
5) C

Lesson Fifty Two

I.

1) May I borrow a cup of sugar?
2) Is your son going to the school play?
3) When should she come over?
4) How many eggs do you need?
5) Can we carpool to work?

收看新唐人

〔新唐人衛星參數〕　位置為東經70.5 度；下載頻率11356.0　；極化垂直；前向糾錯率1/2　；符率4000　。多數地區可用60-90cm的碟形天線接收到。

〔新唐人網路服務〕　新唐人網址為www.ntdtv.com。中國大陸的網友可使用安全加密的“動態網”來正常查閱新唐人網站。發一個短信給以下收件者，幾分鐘內會收到幾個動態網IP：

電子郵件：

d_ip@earthlink.net

（請用海外yahoo　或hotmail　信箱發信）

MSN：

dweb005@hotmail.com

雅虎通：

dweb_ip@yahoo.com

中国各主要城市的天线角度			
城市	天线仰角	天线偏角	天线极化角
沈阳	18.5	63.23	41.73
北京	24.3	58.18	40.67
天津	24.22	59.26	41.81
济南	25.7	60.47	44.27
石家庄	26.78	57.45	41.6
太原	28.25	55.74	40.73
郑州	29.25	58.69	44.58
西安	33.05	54.66	42.38
兰州	35.5	48.08	37
武汉	31	62.1	49.58
长沙	33.26	62.71	51.55
上海	24.68	67.22	52.04
南京	26.57	64.69	50.02
合肥	27.9	63.61	49.54
福州	28.65	68.95	56.96
贵阳	39.49	58.58	49.75
成都	39.05	52.44	42.99
重庆	37.83	55.84	46.02
南昌	30.56	64.67	52.46
广州	35.41	66.94	57.77

- “天線仰角”為接收點天線口平面與鉛垂線的夾角。如為偏饋天線，實際仰角應為計算仰角減天線偏饋角(27.5　度左右)。例如北京仰角為24.3 度 -27.5 度=-3.2 度，天線盤面幾乎跟地面垂直。
- “天線偏角”為接收點天線口平面的垂線與正南方的夾角，向西旋轉為正。
- “極化角”為極化安裝角度與鉛垂線的夾角，面向天線向西旋轉為正。
- 請使用Universal　(10.7-11.7G)的降頻器
- 其他地區資訊請查閱新唐人網站(www.ntdtv.com)

製作:　新唐人電視台
New Tang Dynasty Television
www.ntdtv.com

出版:　開元音像公司
Premier Music & Video, Inc.
229 West 28th Street, Suite 1208
New York, NY 10001, U.S.A.
Tel: 212-967-3088　Fax: 212-967-3077
www.shopping.ntdtv.com

封面設計:　賈紅霞 Joann Xia
封面攝影:　Henry Chen
插畫:　肖平

2007 年 5 月版